Christmas Household Textiles

Jeanette and Donald Michalets

4880 Lower Valley Road Atglen, Pennsylvania 19310

Dedication

This book is dedicated to
Victoria Michalets
who has helped to make so many of our Christmases special for so many years
and to the memory of
Frank Michalets
who was such a loving part of it all.

Published by Schiffer Publishing Ltd.
4880 Lower Valley Road
Atglen, PA 19310
Phone: (610) 593-1777; Fax: (610) 593-2002
E-mail: Info@schifferbooks.com

For the largest selection of fine reference books on this and related subjects, please visit our web site at **www.schifferbooks. com**
We are always looking for people to write books on new and related subjects. If you have an idea for a book please contact us at the above address.

This book may be purchased from the publisher.
Include $3.95 for shipping.
Please try your bookstore first.
You may write for a free catalog.

In Europe, Schiffer books are distributed by
Bushwood Books
6 Marksbury Ave.
Kew Gardens
Surrey TW9 4JF England
Phone: 44 (0) 20 8392-8585; Fax: 44 (0) 20 8392-9876
E-mail: info@bushwoodbooks.co.uk
Website: www.bushwoodbooks.co.uk

Other Schiffer Books by Jeanette Michalets:
Vera Textiles: Add Color to Everyday Fashions
(with Katherine Michalets)

Copyright © 2007 by Jeanette and Donald Michalets
Library of Congress Control Number: 2007923394

Type set in Aldine 721 heading font/text font

ISBN: 978-0-7643-2646-2
Printed in China

Contents

Acknowledgements

Christmas is a time of giving and receiving. We have discovered that writing a book about Christmas textiles is a time of giving and receiving, as well. We wish to thank those friends and family members who gave of themselves to help make this book a reality. We greatly appreciate their loan of Christmas textiles as well as their moral support. Many thanks go to Kirsti Hoffman, Shari Lautenbach, Karen Meer, Ellen Michalets, and Victoria Michalets. Thanks also to Katherine Michalets for love and encouragement, even though she was far away from home.

Introduction

Much of Christmas joy is tied up with sentiment and nostalgia. Advertising, books, movies, and music all play on our love for the Christmas season and the memories it evokes. Famous American artists such as Norman Rockwell and Tasha Tudor created art that specifically reflects the American ideal of Christmas, with its focus on family and the home. Movies such as *It's a Wonderful Life* and *A Christmas Story* have been shown through the years to perpetuate this ideal. Family, friends, church, home, and hearth, these are the stuff of Christmas. Mix in some bright red poinsettias, fragrant balsam, and a jolly old elf in a red suit and . . . there you have it . . . the American Christmas.

Not only have these images been captured in the media, but they have become part of the textiles used in the home to celebrate the holiday. In many homes there is a favorite tablecloth, tree skirt, or wall hanging that has become a treasured part of Christmas holiday decorating. For them, it just would not be Christmas without Grandma's poinsettia-bedecked tablecloth, the gaudy tree skirt covered in sequins, or the table runner that an Aunt so lovingly embroidered.

My Christmas heirloom is a red and white felt Santa Claus mail pouch that my family used to store our Christmas cards before we taped them, one by one, above the living room door. After the cards were hung, the cheery Santa bag brightened a closet door all through the holiday season. Years later, I used it to decorate my first apartment after I was married.

Our collection has grown considerably since the early days of the Santa mail bag. I have added some colorful table runners from the 1930s and a favorite star-shaped doily. I purchased a 1960s round tablecloth and used it as a tree skirt. I began to collect poinsettia-trimmed handkerchiefs. Since beginning to write this book, our collection of vintage Christmas textiles has grown immensely. I never would have guessed there were so many variations on the poinsettia hanky, Christmas-themed tablecloths, or styles of Christmas aprons!

Most of the items shown in this book were found in antique shops during the months of November and December. While collectors may stumble across a few Christmas items throughout the year, the prime months for finding them are late in the year, December being the best time by far. Bargains may be had in January, as well; and at thrift shops, charity shops, and yard sales, Christmas textiles turn up throughout the year. It's a matter of being in the right place at the right time.

Christmas linens and handkerchiefs are also found today at online auction sites, such as eBay. Generally, there are fewer bidders for these items over the summer months, and the items will sell for less cost then than they will closer to the Christmas holiday. Online boutiques provide another source for Christmas textiles, as do estate sales, relatives, and folks who are downsizing their homes.

Pricing

Prices for vintage Christmas textiles are all over the map, as they are for many collectible textiles. It depends on who is selling a piece, where it is being sold, and what the buyer is willing to pay. The old adage still seems to hold true: an item is worth only as much as someone is willing to pay for it.

That said, it does help to have a guide to what dealers are charging for vintage Christmas textiles. I purchased all my textiles in the Midwest, in Wisconsin, and my pricing reflects that. One may expect to pay more on the east and west coasts than in the middle of the country. This seems to hold true for most antiques and collectibles. I based these prices on the items found at antique shops where I purchased most of my collection. For designer items, I used eBay as my guide, as it is difficult to find the nice designer pieces in antique shops. Most of the Tammis Keefe handkerchiefs and Vera tea towels I have were purchased from eBay sellers. I averaged the prices I paid to reach what I consider to be a reasonable middle ground.

Thrift stores are wonderful places to shop, too, especially in the month of December. Prices there are usually quite reasonable. Yard sales are another good source for Christmas linens, especially for shoppers who enjoy the hunt. You may search many yard sales and find nothing, then one day hit the mother lode! To me, this thrill is what hunting for vintage Christmas textiles is all about. Prices are usually quite low at yard sales, sometimes a third of what they would be in an antique shop.

Estate sales are another source that can be found by watching for their advertisements in local newspapers. You often must arrive very early to get the best items.

Family members may also be a source for Christmas linens. When downsizing their homes or apartments, they may wish to part with things they no longer use; and the price is usually right!

All the values given for the items shown in this book are approximate, and should be used only as a guide. The author and publisher do not assume responsibility for losses incurred by the reader while buying or selling vintage Christmas textiles.

What Makes it Vintage?

What constitutes "vintage" is a hot topic of discussion among dealers and collectors these days and everyone seems to have a different opinion! It has been my experience that in the world of textiles and clothing, many dealers consider vintage to mean textiles that date from no later than the 1970s. Some dealers, however, consider even clothing from the 1980s to be vintage, since such clothing is being collected by young buyers. Many of the current fashions shown in magazines are reminiscent of the 1950s – 1980s, with a big emphasis on new interpretations of the styles from the 1960s and 1970s.

For the purpose of this book, I am designating textiles as *vintage* if they are pre-1980. I have included a very few items in the book which date from about 1980, but nearly all the items in the book are older. The oldest textiles in this book date from the late 1920s or early 1930s. The bulk of items are from the 1940s -1960s.

Reader will note that not all the items have an approximate date of origin. There are some items that are just too difficult to date by decade and rather than put a wide range of dates, say ca.1940s-1960s, I have omitted the data for that item. Many Christmas themes were used over a period of decades and it is not always easy to pinpoint the particular decade of origin. Also, most of the textiles in this book were used and no longer have original tags or packaging to help date them. I have employed my own judgement based on knowledge of use of color, fabric, and motif to date the items in this book. My dating is based on educated guesses and is not infallible.

That said, there is certain criteria that I use to date Christmas textiles. Since very little has been written previously about dating vintage Christmas linens, I have used my own observations as a guide. Certain colors and motifs were popular during various decades of the 20th century and this use of color and design extended all the way from advertising and fashion to the fabrics of the decade.

Christmas Colors

When it comes to color, the 1920s and 1930s have a look all their own, which was reflected in the Christmas cards of the era as well as in the textiles. The colors were pure, bold, and dramatic, unlike those of any decade to follow. True red, blue, and yellow were popular on Christmas cards, in the art of children's books, and on textiles. Shades of blue were especially popular and many Christmas cards of the era featured midnight blue backgrounds, often made of foil, as well as blue poinsettias and blue sailing ships.

The color pink was popular in the 1950s and early 1960s and it shows up in the textiles of that era, from pink poinsettias to pink Christmas trees! Later, in the 1960s and 1970s, the colors changed again. Avocado green was sometimes used rather than true, *Christmas green*, and some of the reds had an orange hue.

Christmas Design Motifs

Popular design motifs changed over the decades as well. Many of the designs in the 1920s and 1930s were Art Deco in nature; however, I have found that the Christmas cards and the textiles of that era often harkened back to an earlier day, with their use of people in Colonial dress and village scenes complete with cozy houses, horse-drawn carriages and dogs. Sometimes, the designs of the era mixed the Art Deco with the colonial to produce something entirely new.

The 1940s brought on a traditional look. Traditional Christmas icons decorate the textiles of this time period. Candles, holly, wreaths, pine boughs, poinsettias, and my favorite—bells—are employed liberally on tablecloths, runners and tea towels dating from this period. Occasionally, nearly all of these elements were used in one tablecloth!

The 1950s and 1960s spawned some innovative designers, such as Tammis Keefe, Vera (Vera Neumann), and Robert Darr Wert, whose Christmas designs looked very little like their forerunners. Tammis Keefe, especially, lent a playful air to her work. Her handkerchiefs are whimsical and non-traditional. Her Santa Claus is more than jolly; he is animated and almost mischievous. Her reindeer and her angels have attitude. In addition, her use of color is often different from what had come before and her handkerchiefs often incorporate script in the design. (See the chapter sections on designer handkerchiefs and designer tea towels to learn more.)

The 1970s brought an emphasis on nature and the home. The colors reflected earth tones, especially avocado green and gold. Once again, hearth and home were emphasized.

Materials and Condition

Most of the textiles in this book are made from cotton in some form: pure cotton, cotton linen, cotton felt, and terrycloth. If an article is not cotton, it is designated as "synthetic." This may indicate an item made from nylon, polyester, or another synthetic material. Since most of the items do not have their original tags, a judgment call was made of their compositions, and they are identified as "synthetic".

Most of the items shown in this book are in good-to-mint condition. For the sake of pricing, the standard of *good used condition* is used, meaning the item is basically free of defects such as tears, stains, runs, and color fading. The reader may note that a few items do have some stains or fading, but for the basis of pricing the item they are judged as being in *good used condition.* Some of the handkerchiefs are a bit thin and worn from repeated use and laundering, but this only adds to their charm.

Fabric Care

Christmas linens are relatively easy to care for. Being mostly cotton, they are machine washable and may be dried in a machine dryer. Felt items should not be washed, for they will be ruined. Delicate items should be laundered on gentle or hand-wash settings or be washed by hand in a sink. Most tea towels and handkerchiefs can be ironed on the cotton setting of an electric pressing iron, but do test the item on a cooler setting when you start. Be mindful of not scorching or tearing delicate lace trim.

Textile items should be stored flat, and the best ones should be placed between sheets of acid-free tissue paper. It is especially important to store handkerchiefs flat, since over time folded creases become almost permanent and yellowing will occur along fold lines. The same caution holds true for tablecloths, table runners, and tea towels. Store your textile items where they are safe from moths, mice, and other pests.

Keep brightly colored textiles out of the sun, and if you frame a piece use acid-free glass and hang it where the sun won't cause damage.

Using Your Textiles

There are many ways to use vintage Christmas textiles. I use a favorite round tablecloth as a tree skirt, for example. This tablecloth dates from about the 1960s and features colonial people and horse-drawn sleighs. It is trimmed in white fringe. I like the cheery look of it, especially on the days before it gets buried under gifts. The nice thing about a cotton tree skirt is that it can be cleaned in a washing machine after the holiday. One cannot do that with felt.

I also enjoy displaying some of my favorite tea towels in my dining room on a linen rack. The hard part is deciding which ones to display! It is fun to rotate my collection each year. Tea towels can be hung in the kitchen for use or just to be admired, it is your choice. Also, they can be placed down the center of a table, as a runner, or on a computer keyboard as protection against dust.

Festive aprons also can be worn or displayed. A small ladder hung on a wall makes a great display rack for aprons. Simply tie the aprons to the rungs in an eye-pleasing manner organized by color, material, or design. Small aprons can even be strung across a large window as a Christmas curtain.

Tablecloths may be used on tables throughout the house as well as in the dining room. Rotate them on your kitchen table and use small ones on side tables and under tabletop Christmas trees and decorations.

If you have a glass-covered coffee table, you can display handkerchiefs under the glass. A collage can be made from handkerchiefs alone, or they can be mixed with vintage Christmas cards. A glass-topped dressing table is another place to show off hankies. Try putting handkerchiefs on a bathroom shelf. Lacy handkerchiefs or those with poinsettias can be placed under perfume bottles and displayed in baskets. The same may be done in the dining room by tucking lace-trimmed hankies into long-stem glasses or glass baskets. Hankies can also be used as doilies on a buffet table.

Just imagine all the wonderful things you can make from fabulous vintage Christmas fabric. Some designs never go out of style. If you love to sew, consider making a holiday quilt from vintage Christmas handkerchiefs. A Christmas quilt can be created with many patterns of the same type or with a variety of holiday patterns. Magazines and craft books often provide instructions for making holiday quilts. With a little imagination, the possibilities are endless!

One of the great benefits of vintage Christmas linens is their ability to be fun to collect and a pleasure to use. Happy hunting!

PREPARATIONS

Lightweight cotton fabric with a colonial scene. $10-12.

Tea Towels

Dishing It Up

There are so many terrific tea towels, certainly something to suit every taste. I am partial to their cheery, mid-twentieth-century motifs. And they launder so well in the washing machine. I would like to say I have a favorite, but it is difficult to pick just one!

Santa peers through a green wreath. Border of candy canes and ornaments. "Noel" is printed above the wreaths. Ca. 1960s. $13-18.

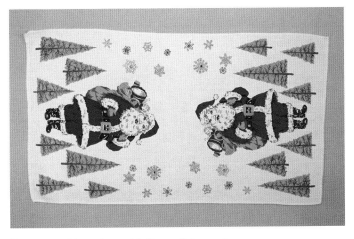

Santa totes his pack on this linen dish towel. Ca. 1960s/1970s. $13-18.

Santa's Coming to Town

Could St. Nick get any jollier?

Jolly Santas and pretty poinsettias. Ca. 1960s. $13-18.

A jolly Santa rides in his sleigh on this towel with the look of cross-stitch. Tag reads: *Parisian Prints. All Pure Linen*. Ca. 1970s. $13-18.

Noel . . . Noel . . .

Printing the word "Noel" and other holiday greetings on tea towels was fashionable in the 1950s and '60s. Not all of these towels share these sentiments, but they are all bright and cheery.

Terry towel. Red, green, and yellow towel features a Christmas tree and fireplace. Border of ornaments and candy canes. "Noel" in red letters. Ca. 1960s. $12-15.

Bell and poinsettia motif on this terry towel, along with the word, "Noel". Ca. 1950s/1960s. $12-15.

Red birds sing, "Noel Noel" on this colorful terrycloth towel with a sleepy Santa and a clock. $12-15.

Red and green ornaments adorn evergreen boughs tied with red bows on this linen towel. Ca.1950s/1960s. $13-18.

A pair of wreaths are garnished with fruit. Linen. $13-18.

This festive tea towel has it all: reindeer, candles, Santa Claus, Christmas trees, and poinsettias. Cotton linen. Ca.1950s/1960s. $15-25.

Red candles in old-fashioned lanterns. Tag reads: *Fallani & Cohn. All linen.* Ca. 1950s/1960s. $15-20.

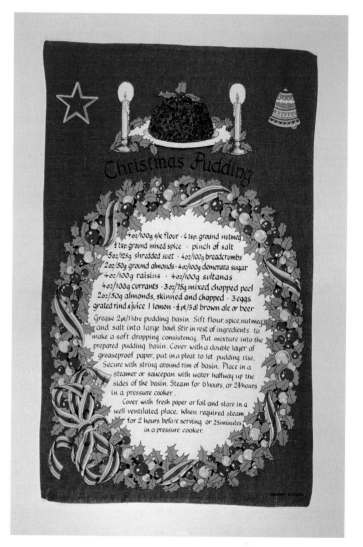

This delightful towel features a Christmas Pudding recipe. Sheriff Textiles. Ca. 1970s. $15-20.

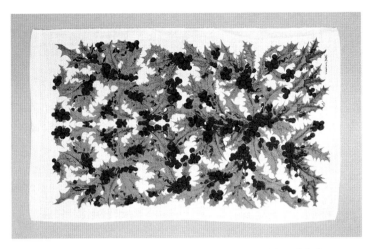

Green holly leaves and red berries. Signed, "Marge French". Screen printed by *Kay Dee*. Linen. Ca. 1960s/1970s. $15-20.

Deep red poinsettias. Hand printed by *Kay Dee*. $13-18.

Candy canes, bells, and bows. Ca. 1950s/1960s. $13-18.

Deep red poinsettias surrounded by a gold border. $13-18.

Designer Delights

Some well known textile designers created Christmas linens. Tammis Keefe, Vera Neumann, and Robert Darr Wert are among them. They all used bold, modern designs and innovative colors. They took traditional motifs, such as angels, poinsettias, and Christmas trees, and rendered them in new ways.

Tammis Keefe

Towel designs by Tammis Keefe display her modernistic approach to angels and her penchant for script.

Tammis Keefe signed towel. Stylish angels cavort on this distinctive towel. Note the word "Noel" on the angel's apron. Ca. 1950s. $30-40.

Another Tammis Keefe design. Cherubim and music decorate this pretty towel. Ca. 1950s. $30-40.

Vera

Prolific artist and textile designer Vera Neumann, better known simply as Vera, was well known for innovative and affordable garments, scarves, table linens, bed linens, kitchen linens, and much more. Most of her work is signed with her first name. Many of her signed pieces have a ladybug before or after her signature. Vera chose the ladybug symbol because it suggests "happiness" in many parts of the world. Vera's tea towels are bright and happy. Her poinsettias are particularly abstract. She frequently included ferns and mushrooms in her designs.

Vera. Abstract poinsettia on green ground. Lady bug logo. Ca. 1960s/1970s. $18-22.

Designed by Vera. Stylish "modern" poinsettias on ivory-colored background. Signed, "Vera" with the lady bug logo. Ca. 1960s/1970s. $18-22.

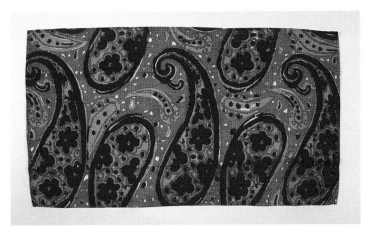

Vera. Red and green paisley. No signature, but tag states: *Vera. Linen*. Ca. 1960s/1970s. $13-18.

Vera. Red and white poinsettias on a red ribbon. Lady bug logo. Ca. 1960s/1970s. $18-22.

Robert Darr Wert

Artist Robert Darr Wert worked in the middle of the twentieth century. He created designs for ceramic tile, as well as textiles. Some of his work features elements of nature. His tiles often incorporate plants in their designs. For example, Wert used ferns and mushrooms on a tile design he called "Woodland Walk." Another tile is called "Herbs." Here, Wert incorporated recipes and herb bottles in the design.

Designer Knock-offs

Other tea towels were created to look like designer pieces, but are not signed. The angel with tall hair is reminiscent of Tammis Keefe's work, and the towel with many ornaments reminds one of Robert Darr Wert's tea towels with numerous, brightly colored objects scattered across it.

"Christmas Kitchen" signed by artist Robert Darr Wert. This cheerful design depicts many holiday elements. The towel is edged with the words, "Deck the halls with boughs of holly, fa la la la la." Ca. 1950s/1960s. $25-35.

A designer look-alike. Shades of pink, red, and green date this charming towel to the 1950s/1960s. Label reads: Pure linen. $22-28.

Reminiscent of Tammis Keefe and Vera, this towel
is a darling knock-off. Ca. 1950s/1960s. $20-30.

Jazzy ornaments make this tea towel pop. Ca. 1960s. $20-25.

Hand Painted and Embroidered Tea Towels

These towels feature hand-painted and delicately embroidered designs. Busy hands make pretty towels.

Green tree with embroidered trim on white cotton. *Courtesy of Kirsti Hoffman.* $7-10.

Bells with embroidered trim on white cotton. *Courtesy of Kirsti Hoffman.* $7-10.

An angel flies over a little town on this cute embroidered piece. $6-10.

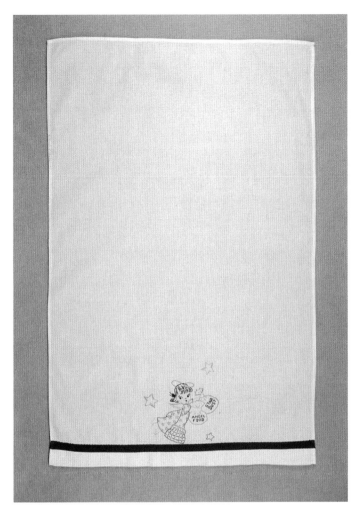

A cute little angel carries bags of "angel food" and "star dust'. Embroidered. $6-8.

Tea towel embroidered with poinsettias. Large size. $6-8.

The handsome Santa Claus is actually a dish cloth set. He's just too cute to use for ketchup spills and grungy pots and pans. I guess that's why he is still in his original package!

Santa kitchen towel set. Santa is made of dish cloths. Original box and label. Made by "Hanson." Chenille button nose. Ca. 1960s. $20-25.

Terry Towels and Hot Pads

Terrycloth hand towels are fun and they brighten any kitchen at Christmas time. They come with a myriad of motifs.

Ornaments and Bells

These towels are decorated with ornaments and bells. The ornaments towel is a Vera design.

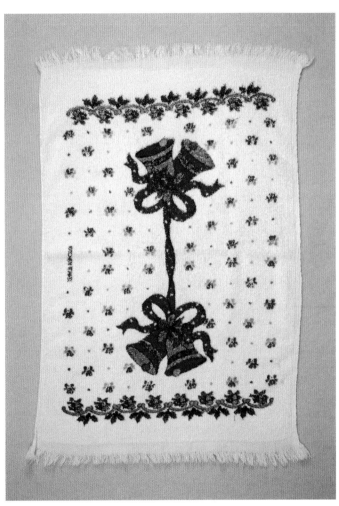

Joyous bells ring on this terry cloth towel. $6-8.

Red, green, and peach-colored ornaments. Terry cloth. Vera tag. Ca. 1960s/1970s. $16-20.

Santa and Company

Cute Kris Kringles and chubby snowmen bring these terry towels to life.

Santa and Christmas tree. Gold trim. Ca. 1960s. $6-10.

A musical snowman and Santa Claus bring wishes of " Merry Christmas" and "Happy New Year." Ca. 1960s. $10-12.

A jolly snowman shovels snow. Ca. 1960s. $6-10.

Three snowmen carry a sign that says, " Season's Greetings."
Ca. 1960s. $8-12.

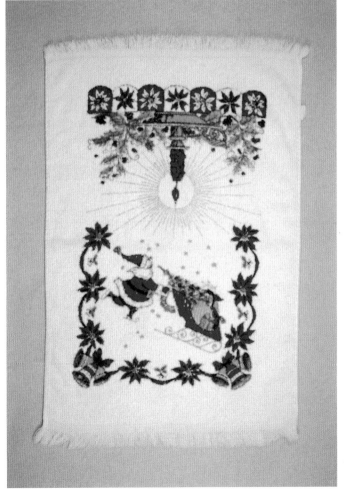

Santa pushes a sleigh of goodies on this terry towel. Ca. 1960s. $6-10.

1950s Pink

These wonderful little hand towels might brighten a powder room. Pink was a popular color in the 1950s, as seen in the pink-clad Santa Claus on the Christmas card.

Good Things to Eat

What could be yummier than home-baked cookies or crispy gingerbread men?

Small towel with red and pink ornaments. "Merry Christmas" in green letters. Ca. 1950s/1960s. $6-10.

Holiday messages form the background for this yummy design of cookies, candy canes, and nuts. Ca. 1970s. $6-8.

Pink and red bells decorate this towel with sentiments for the new year. Ca. 1950s/1960s. $6-10.

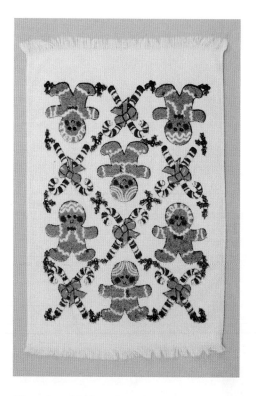

Gingerbread kids and candy canes. Ca. 1970s. $6-8.

Glowing Lights

Candles add warmth to these terry towels.

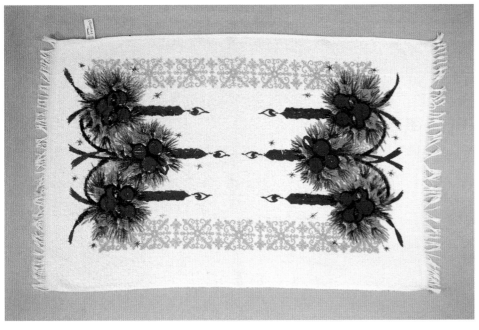

Large red candles, greens, and red ornaments. Tag reads: *Terries by Sintex. All cotton. Made in U.S.A.* Ca. 1960s. $8-10.

This towel has a crocheted top with a button so that it may be fastened on a cabinet or oven door. Ca.1970s. $4-6.

Yellow lanterns illuminate this towel that offers, "Greetings." Ca.1970s. $8-10.

More Poinsettias

Here are some fabric poinsettias to brighten the kitchen.

A bath-sized towel. Tag reads: *Style House. All Cottton. Montgomery Ward.* Ca.1960s. $7-10.

Bright poinsettias and green leaves. Ca. 1970s. $6-8.

Hot Pads and Mitts

Even hot pads and kitchen mitts were made with Christmas themes!

These sweet crocheted hot pads are not strictly Christmas in their designs, but their cheery red and white colors work well at the holidays. The little dresses and pantaloons are too cute to use; they remain favorite decorations.

Although not strictly for Christmas, these adorable hot pads add a festive air to kitchen décor at the holidays. Crocheted. Very collectible. $8-12 each.

Another crocheted cutie in the form of pantaloons. $8-12.

These cotton hot mitts probably date from the 1960s or '70s. Holly Hobby™ still has her original store tags.

Santa waves hello. Ca.1970s. $6-10.

Two festive crocheted hot pads hang from a Christmasy hanger. $15-20, the set.

Crocheted hot pad with poinsettia motif. $4-6.

Holly Hobby™ hot pad with original tag. From American Greetings. Ca. 1970s. $6-8.

This hot pad coordinates with a hand towel. $4-6.

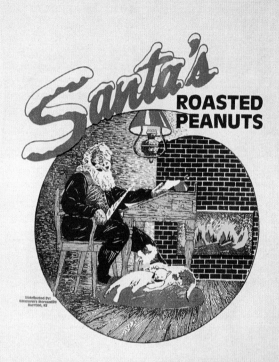

Peanut bag. Unusual large cotton sack advertises "Santa's Roasted Peanuts. From Red's Peanut Farm." Dog and cat lie at Santa's feet. $30-35.

Home Decorations

Felt Crafts

Women's magazines encouraged homemakers to create their own Christmas decorations with "how-to" directions they supplied for many items, from advent calendars to stockings and tree skirts. Generally, many of these decorations were made from felt and lavishly embellished with sequins. They were simple and relatively inexpensive to make.

Even celebrities were called upon to get crafty at holiday time. The Lennon Sisters singing group, of television's The Lawrence Welk Show fame, busily made Christmas crafts and appeared on the cover of *Lady's Circle* in 1972. "Dad's" stocking, complete with toes, and the stocking shaped like an old-time lady's boot with daisy buttons are some of the quirkiest felt stockings to be found.

Directions for making felt advent calendars with candies attached. From *Better Homes & Gardens Christmas Ideas for 1964.*

The Lennon Sisters display their crafting talents on the cover of *Lady's Circle,* December, 1972.

A felt calendar with little charms, to make at home. *Better Homes & Gardens Christmas Ideas for 1964.*

Article about making felt stockings. *Better Homes & Gardens Christmas Ideas for 1962.*

Felt stocking pattern. Jolly snowmen trim this pattern for a large red stocking. $5-7.

This homemade stocking was made just for Mom. $7-10.

Handmade felt "Dad" stocking. $7-12.

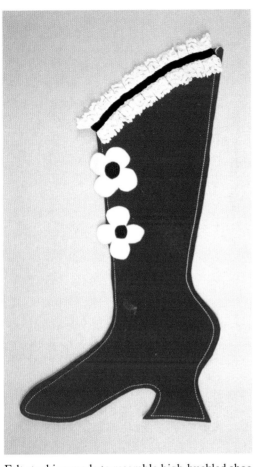

Felt stocking made to resemble high-buckled shoe. Daisy "buttons." $7-12.

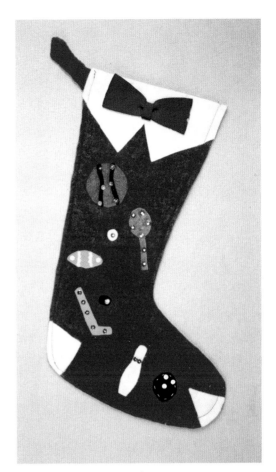

Sports-themed stocking. $7-12.

Felt stocking with silver glitter trim. Homemade. $7-12.

A patchwork Holly Hobby™ look-a-like decorates this felt stocking. Ca. 1970s. $7-10.

Magazine features felt banners. *Better Homes & Gardens Christmas Ideas for 1962.*

Felt door or wall hanging spells out, "Noel". $6-8.

Handmade felt banner reads, "Merry Christmas" in French. Oops! The letters in "Joyeux Noel" have strange spacing. $8-10.

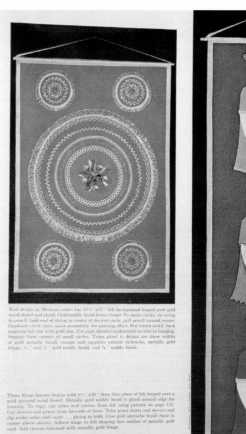

Crafty wall banners made of felt, sequins, and bric-a-brac. *Better Homes & Gardens Christmas Ideas for 1964.*

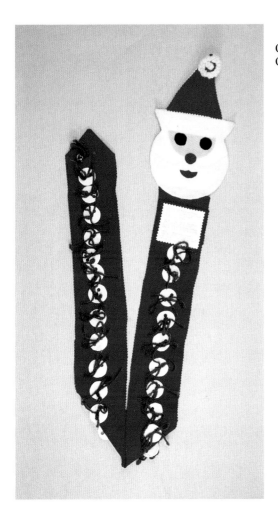

Cute felt Santa with Christmas poem. $10-12.

Detail of Santa's face and poem.

Magazine article touts, "No sew with rick-rack trims." *Better Homes & Gardens, Christmas Ideas for 1964.*

Felt Christmas tree with sequin ornaments $7-10.

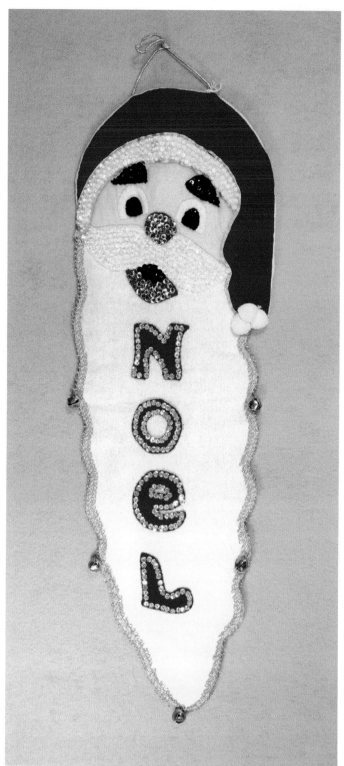

Felt Santa with "Noel" on his beard. $10-12.

Funky Santa and reindeer wall hanging covered in sequins. $15-20.

These felt toilet seat covers are something else! They are so wonderfully tacky it is no wonder Santa is hiding his face.

Toilet seat cover. Santa face appears on this somewhat tacky textile. White pompom trim. Felt. $10-15.

Another toilet seat cover. This one has Santa going down the pipes . . . er . . . chimney. $10-15.

A modest Santa hides his eyes on the back side of the toilet seat cover.

I love these banners. They are so nostalgic and the one where we see Santa through a key hole is so clever. They just don't make things like this anymore.

Tablerunner. Felt with jolly Santa, gifts, and candy canes on each end. Sequins and braid trim. $15-20.

Old tapestry depicts an elf-like Santa Claus trimming the tree while three children peek through keyhole. Tree is trimmed with sequins and beads. Ca.1940s/1950s. $20-25.

More Home Decorations

Another item looks like a doll bib, but it isn't. It's a dish soap bottle cover! It is the first one I have ever seen. Even dish soap needs to look stylish at Christmas time.

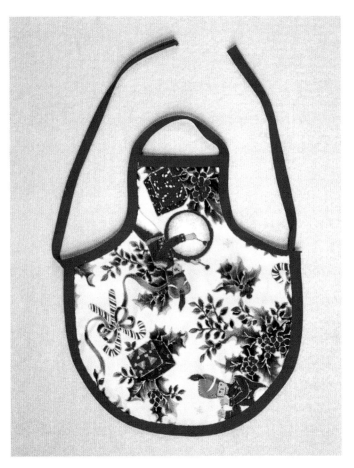

No, it's not a tiny bib—it's a dish soap bottle cover! Cotton with Christmas print. $4-6.

Silky tapestry with gold fringe wishes "Merry Christmas and a Happy New Year." $20-25.

Fabric. Red poinsettias, pine cones, and berries. Note the red geraniums in the design. Fringed edge. Cotton. $12-15.

Aprons

Mama's Holiday Finery

Aprons were popular accessories in the middle of the twentieth century, both the useful kitchen styles and the fancy ornamental ones. A mid-century Mom wouldn't think of preparing a Christmas dinner without a pretty apron to protect her good dress. Today, some of these little vintage beauties are too pretty to wear!

Popular women's magazines of the 1950s and '60s often featured designs and patterns to make Christmas aprons.

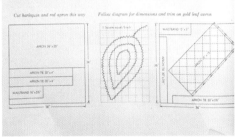

A homemaker tries to choose among three holiday aprons. Apron "how-to" page from *Better Homes & Gardens Christmas Ideas for 1959.*

This pretty miss shows off her fancy red apron. The other two are equally stylish in shades of green and gold. *Better Homes & Gardens Christmas Ideas for 1959.*

This page from the magazine shows many apron patterns. The one in the second row, right, is featured in this book. *Better Homes & Gardens Christmas Ideas for 1959.*

This apron definitely has a Christmas theme. Santa emerges from a large chimney. The bottom portion of the apron is designed to look like a house. Note the very "space age" coffee pot! *Better Homes & Gardens Christmas Ideas for 1959.*

Glad Tidings We Bring . . .

These aprons bring glad tidings in several languages.

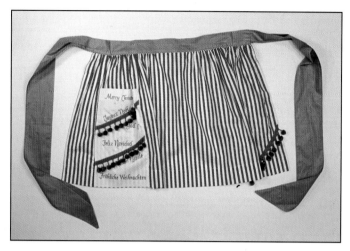

This apron wishes "Merry Christmas" in French, Norwegian, Spanish, Italian, and German. Green pompoms add a jaunty touch. $12-15.

Cute Santas and snowmen decorate pink candles on this terrycloth apron. Who wouldn't have a Merry Christmas and a Happy New Year wearing this little cutie. Ca. 1950s. $15-20.

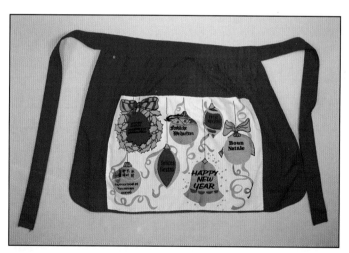

"Merry Christmas" in several languages on ornaments of many shapes. Treated cotton. Ca. 1960s. $12-15.

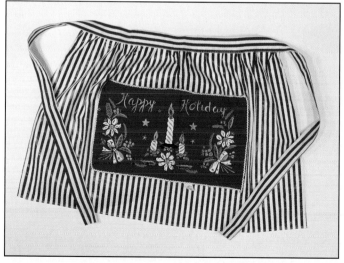

"Happy Holiday" is spelled out in gold and black letters on the large pocket of this striped apron. Cotton. Ca. 1960s. $10-15.

Many different motifs are featured on Christmas aprons. A few of the aprons featured here are handmade with embroidery or bric-a-brac trim. Notice the apron with a handkerchief sewn on it. Apron fabrics range from cotton to terry cloth and nylon.

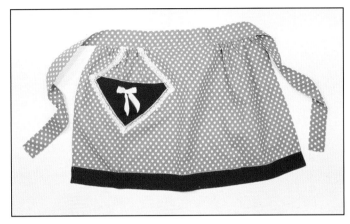

Polka dot cotton fabric trimmed with lace and ribbon. Ca.1960s. $10-15.

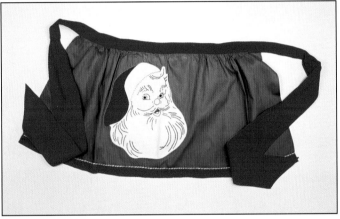

Blue-eyed felt Santa is front and center on this pristine cotton apron. Ca. 1950s/1960s. $15-20.

Santa apron with terry cloth towel attached. Cotton. Ca. 1960s. $15-20.

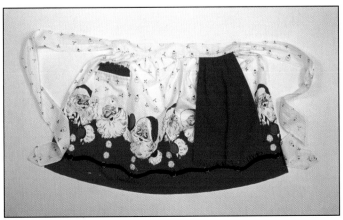

Homemade cotton apron made with a tea towel. Ca. 1960s. $10-15.

Cotton apron with turquoise and pink houses and old-fashioned people. Ca.1950s. $12-16.

Homemade cotton apron with bric-a-brac. $8-12.

Sexy little satin apron with mesh overskirt. Green ribbon bows and bead trim. Ca. 1950s/1960s. $12-18.

The pocket on this apron is a present. " Mom" is embroidered on the gift. Very sweet. Cotton. $15-20.

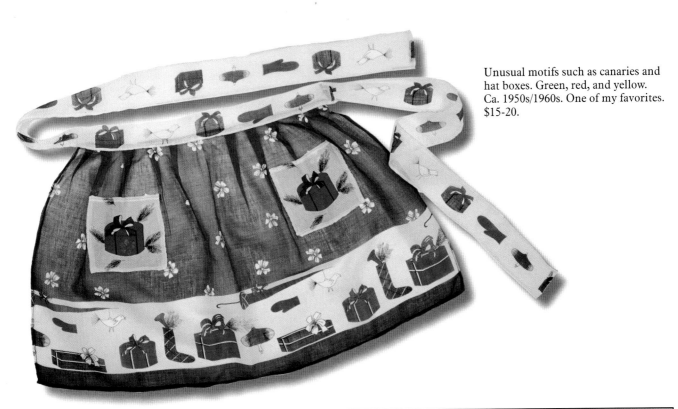

Unusual motifs such as canaries and hat boxes. Green, red, and yellow. Ca. 1950s/1960s. One of my favorites. $15-20.

A cute terry cloth piece with original label. A stamped design of colonial carolers, bells, ornaments, etc. Tag reads: *Hand Printed. Kitchen Companions. All Cotton. Made in U.S.A.* Ca. 1960s. $15-20.

Bric-a-brac trims this simple cotton apron. $8-10.

Lively trees with pink, red, and green ornaments. Note the candles on the trees. Ca.1950s/1960s. $12-18.

This organdy, handmade apron is trimmed with a large handkerchief that was cut in half. $12-16.

Bells, ornaments and other motifs decorate this cotton apron. Ca. 1950s. $8-12.

A sheer apron with unusual yellow border and waist band. Ca.1960s. $15-20.

Pretty red and green apron depicts Santa with candy cane and toys. Colorful trim and waist band. Ca. 1950s/1960s. *Courtesy of Shari Lautenbach.* $15-20.

Cute checked design. Cotton. Ca. 1960s. $12-18.

Wreaths of holly and red ribbon enliven this lightweight, home-sewn apron. $10-15.

Sheer organdy with red waist band. Gold and red bells on gold rope trimmed with holly. Ca. 1960s. $10-15.

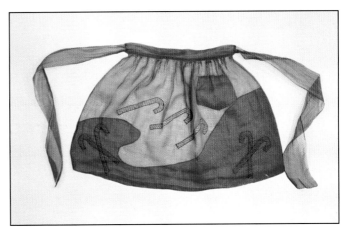

Red and white candy canes on green. $8-12.

Santa and Christmas tree appliqued on this cotton apron. Ca. 1960s. $12-16.

Organdy apron with "modern" tree design. Ca. 1960s/1970s. $10-15.

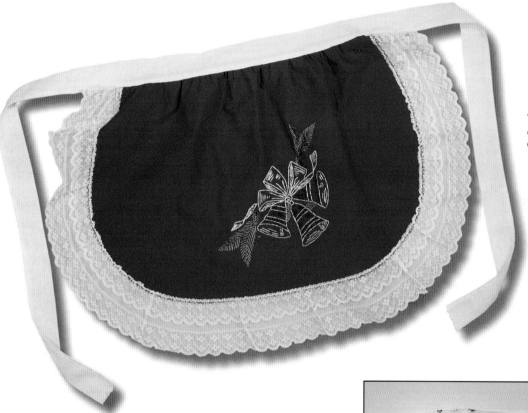

This lace-trimmed cutie features embroidered bells and pine cones. Ca.1950s/1960s. $10-15.

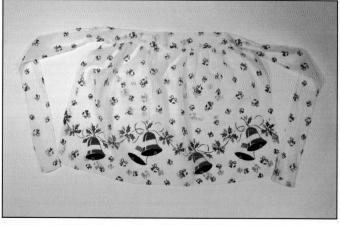

Yellow and red bells on sheer cotton. Ca.1940s. $10-15.

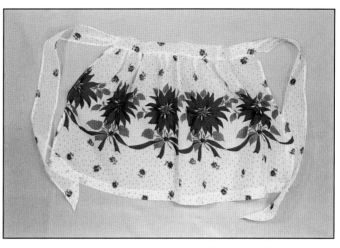

Large poinsettias and red ribbon. Cotton. Ca. 1960s. $10-15.

Red, white, and green bands trim the waist and the hem of this apron. Cotton. $7-10.

Hand made apron with bric-a-brac on the pocket, waist, and hem. Cotton. $8-12.

Hand made felt apron with gold cord and lots of sequins. Gros grain ribbon ties. $10-15.

Cross-stitched cutie from 1976. Note the creator's signature, "Mary" and the date, "12-25-76 embroidered in the right corner. Cotton. $10-15.

Slim potted Christmas trees and candy canes on this cotton apron. $10-15.

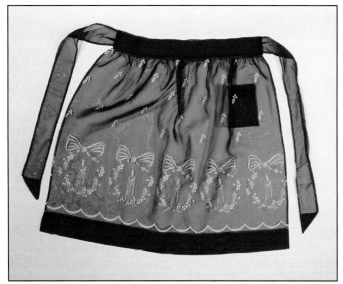

Nylon with raised wreath and candle design. $8-12.

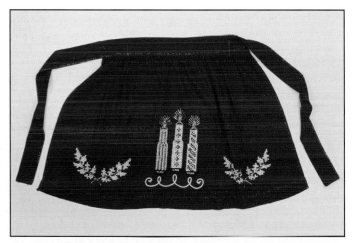

Candles and branches cross-stitched on red. Gold trim. Cotton. $10-15.

Sheer Organdy

Some of the daintiest aprons are made from organdy fabric. They are pretty enough to wear all through dinner!

Sheer organdy with lovely embroidered holly design. $10-15.

Colorful designs of trees, snow-men, candy canes, and birds. Green stars on white background. Ca. 1960s. $15-20.

Sheer organdy with large felt candle trimmed with sequins. Embroidered details. Ca. 1960s. $10-15.

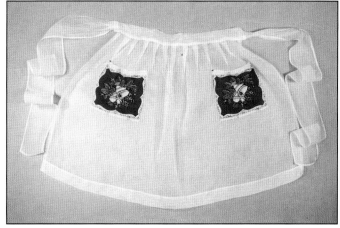

Large pockets with bell design add color to this sheer apron. Ca. 1950s. $10-15.

49

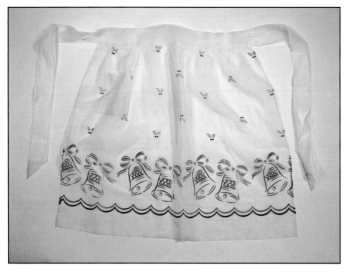

Sheer organdy apron with red and green bells. Ca.1950s/1960s. $10-12.

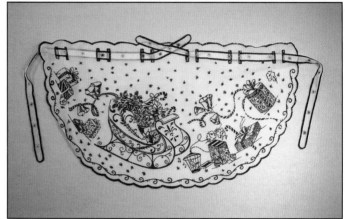

Chenille sleigh, birdcage, and gift boxes enliven this sweet little number. Ca. 1950s/1960s. $15-18.

Sheer organdy apron with embroidered poinsettia and gold bric-a-brac. $8-10.

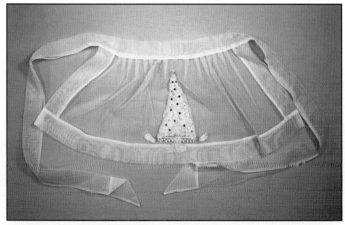

Dainty sheer nylon apron decorated with white tree and pink ribbon gifts. Ca. 1950s. $10-15.

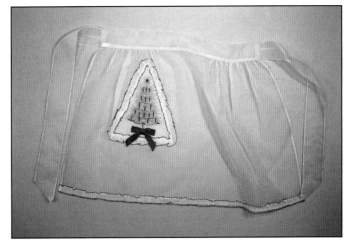

Darling organdy apron embroidered with Christmas tree. Red lace and a big bow. Ca. 1950s/1960s. $10-15.

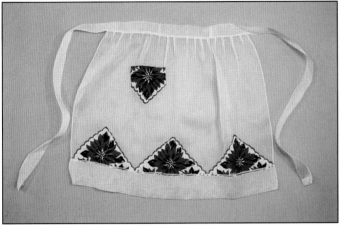

Hand sewn. Triangles of poinsettia-printed material decorate this piece. Ca. 1960s. $8-10.

Lightweight apron with poinsettias and ribbon. $10-12.

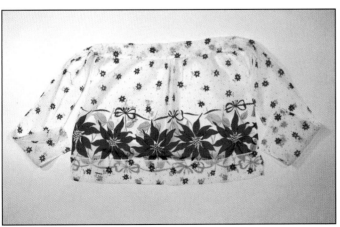

Sheer poinsettia-trimmed apron. $8-12.

Pink accents make this apron different. Ca.1950s/1960s. $10-15.

Green holly leaves on pocket. Tag reads: *Carmen Lee. All cotton exclusive of decoration.* Ca. 1960s. $8-10.

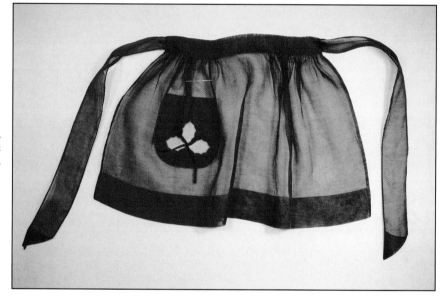

Cute Santas spell out "Merry Christmas" on this funky apron. Ca. 1960s. $10-15.

Gingham Girl

Cotton gingham gives these aprons a homespun, practical feel. The apron with the two large deer is distinctive.

Cross-stitched poinsettias on tan checked material. Cotton. $10-15.

Cross-stitched poinsettias on gray checked cotton. $10-15.

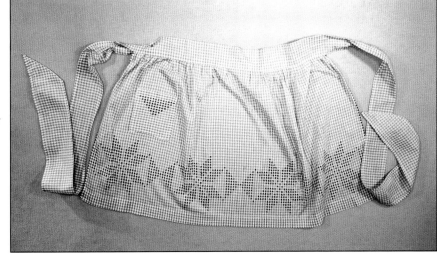

Large apron with elegant cross-stitched deer. $15-18.

Red gingham with snowflake pattern. $10-15.

Cross-stitched trees on gingham apron. $10-15.

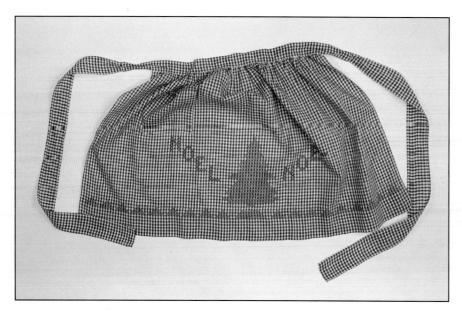

Christmas trees and the word, "Noel' cross-stitched on red gingham. $10-15.

Full-length Styles

A Few Christmas aprons were made in full length. These date from the late 1970s to about 1980, when long dresses were popular casual styles.

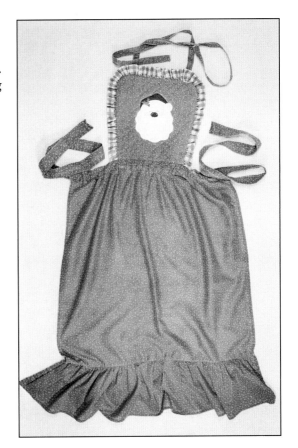

Felt Santa on full-length green apron. Ca. 1980. $10-12.

Homemade full-length apron. Small quilted squares embellish the bodice of this apron. Note the fabric trims near the hem. Ca. 1980. $10-12.

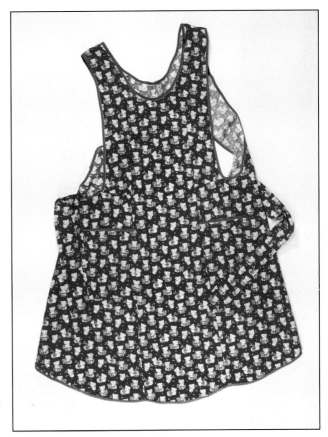

Full length apron with cute little bears on boxes and baubles. Ca. 1970s. $10-12.

Scarves and Accessories

These cotton scarves have Christmas holiday themes. The scarf with a winter scene is the oldest one, and not strictly for Christmas, but it could be used all winter long.

Child's scarf with religious theme. 50% cotton. 50% polyester. Made in U.S.A. Ca. 1970s. $6-8.

Nostalgic winter scene on this large, cotton scarf. Red fringe border. Ca. 1950s. $15-20.

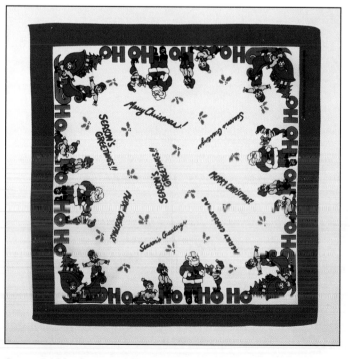

Santa and his elves say, " Ho, ho, ho" and send season's greetings. Cotton and polyester. Ca. 1970s. $6-8.

Men need some Christmas finery, too. The magazine advertisement is from the 1940s.

Coca Cola™ necktie. Polar bear enjoys a Coke™ by his Christmas tree. $8-$12.

Christmas Seals necktie. $10-15.

Magazine ad from *Holiday* magazine, December, 1950. Note the pretty female image used to sell the ties.

Handkerchiefs

A Hankering for Hankies

Handkerchiefs are a pleasure to collect all year round, but there is something special about the holiday ones. In Grandma's day, one could not imagine going anywhere without a crisp white handkerchief tucked in one's pocket or purse. In addition to the ubiquitous white handkerchief, hankies were designed with flower, animal, and holiday motifs, with Christmas designs seemingly the most common. Some handkerchiefs were stitched with fine embroidery and others were machine-made with printed designs. Handkerchiefs were manufactured with lace trim, with crocheted edges, and with monograms. Some of the loveliest and most desirable hankies are those dating from the 1800s or early 1900s. These handkerchiefs are usually white with fine lace or embroidery.

Most of the handkerchiefs in this book date from the middle of the twentieth century when colorful and whimsically designed handkerchiefs were at the peak of their popularity. By about 1960, handkerchiefs were on their way out, with most folks opting for the ease and cleanliness of disposable tissues; however, handkerchiefs continued to be manufactured in the 1960s and some of the very pretty poinsettia designs in this book date from that era. Most of these handkerchiefs were made in the Philippines. The majority of the embroidered white handkerchiefs featured in the book were produced in Switzerland.

Of course, handkerchiefs were intended as fashion accessories. Why not carry one in your purse instead of generic facial tissues? Tuck one in a suit or jacket pocket. Pin one with a pretty broach to your lapel, if you are daring.

Child's Play

Children's Christmas handkerchiefs are much harder to find than ones intended for adults and, therefore, generally cost more. It is likely that Children's hankies did not survive the wear and tear children gave them. They are generally smaller in size than adult handkerchiefs, measuring about 8" or 9" square. They feature bold colors and themes such as angels, Santa Claus, and toys. The two Burmel hankies I have included in this section, are not necessarily only for children and are larger in size. I do believe the charming cat and dog designs would appeal to children and adults, alike.

Adorable angels and stars on green ground. Cotton. Ca.1950. $10-15.

Angels play with toys. Made in Germany. Small size. Cotton. Ca. 1950s-1960s. $10-15.

Angelic children bake cookies and pies. German. Small size. Cotton. Ca.1950s-1960. $10-15.

Elephant, horse, and jack-in-the-box at North Pole. Hanky reads: Toys of the World. Small size. Cotton. Ca.1950s-1960s. $8-10.

Santa checks his list. Santa figure is hand painted. Cotton. Ca.1950s-1960s. $8-10.

Cute kittens in red boots with ornaments, bells, and candy canes. Made by Burmel. Large size. Tag reads: Handkerchief of the month by Burmel, as seen in Vogue. Ca.1960. $15-18.

Scottie dog wearing red bow sits beneath Christmas tree. Burmel. Large. $15-18.

Designer Delights

The first three handkerchiefs in this section were designed by the very talented and whimsical textile designer, Tammis Keefe. Ms. Keefe's unique approach to color and design brought a fresh, contemporary feel to her creations. Her work was playful and animated. Her Santa Claus and reindeer seem to leap from the fabric. Tammis Keefe was a contemporary of Vera Neumann and Faith Austin and there are some similarities among their designs. One of the things that distinguish Ms. Keefe's work from that of her contemporaries is the use of lettering and script on many of her handkerchiefs and tea towels. Her color palette was consistent with the 1950s: pink, turquoise, chartreuse, and black.

Tammis Keefe's designs sell well on the Internet. She appears to be highly sought after and collectors are paying high prices for her designs. Because Ms. Keefe died in 1960 at the tender age of 32, there may be less of her work available than that of her contemporaries, although she was quite prolific. Her designs are signed, "Tammis Keefe" in relatively small script. The "S" in her signature is bigger than the other letters and I have seen her name mistakenly written as "Tammi S Keefe."

Tammis Keefe. Unusual colors of lime green and pink. *Merry Christmas* in white and pink script. Pink snowflake. Ca.1950-1960. $15-20.

Tammis Keefe. Cheerful red and green hanky. *Merry Christmas* in white script around border. Ca. 1950-1960. $18-25.

This little cutie was designed by another talented designer, Pat Pritchard. Each little square contains a different image.

Pat Prichard. Intricate hanky features angels, ornaments, a cake stand, a bird and a candy jar. Small size. Ca.1950-1960. $15-18.

Sentimental Favorites

White handkerchiefs with embroidered designs were popular all year round, in their day, and were often given boxed as gifts. Many elementary school teachers received an embroidered hanky or two at the annual Christmas party. Pretty and inexpensive, they could be tucked into an envelope and mailed with a Christmas card.

One could never go wrong with the gift of an embroidered handkerchief; it was always in good taste. The ones featured in this section are each embroidered with sentiments, such as "Season's Greetings" and "Merry Christmas." The green handkerchief was probably a souvenir brought to the United States from England.

Embroidered *Seasons Greetings* on holly leaves. $4-6.

Embroidered *Seasons Greetings* between poinsettias. $4-6.

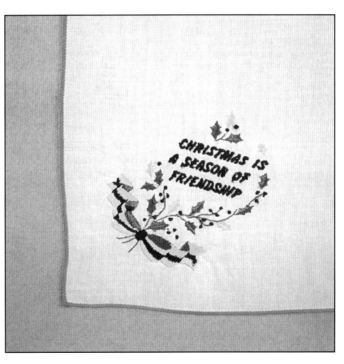

Ivy tied with green and red ribbon. Reads: *Christmas is a Season of Friendship*. $5-7.

Elegant Embroidery

These handkerchiefs are embroidered with images from poinsettias and Christmas trees to candles, bells, and Santa Claus. Embroidered hankies make up a big portion of collectible handkerchiefs. They may still be purchased reasonably and collectors appreciate their sentimental appeal. Especially prized are the ones with lace edges.

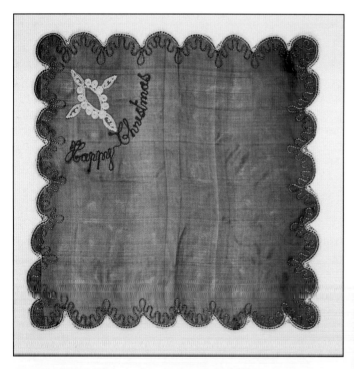

Merry Christmas embroidered above a wreath with bell. Made in Switzerland. $5-7.

Santa brings gifts and a Christmas tree. Tag reads: All cotton. Made in Switzerland. Desco. $5-7.

English. *Happy Christmas* in red thread in one corner. Pink embroidered design. Scalloped edge. Synthetic. $10-12.

Delicate lace borders this hanky with an embroidered poinsettia and a wreath in one corner. Label reads: All cotton. Treasure Masters. Made in Switzerland. $5-7.

Embroidered with lantern and green boughs. $5-7.

Design of red bell with holly and leaves. Tag reads: All Cotton. Made in Switzerland. Desco. $5-7.

Small tree in corner. Red edging. $4-6.

Stem of red and white poinsettias. Tag reads: All cotton. Made in Switzerland. $5-7.

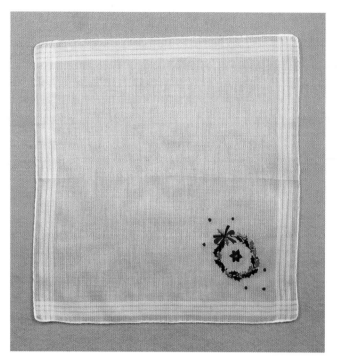

Corner design of wreath with pink and red bow. $4-6.

Unusual design of candelabrum and poinsettias. $5-7.

Three clusters of red bells and holly. $5-7.

Pretty red bell. Tag reads: All cotton. Made in Switzerland. $5-7.

Lace edge. Red poinsettia. White ribbon. $5-7.

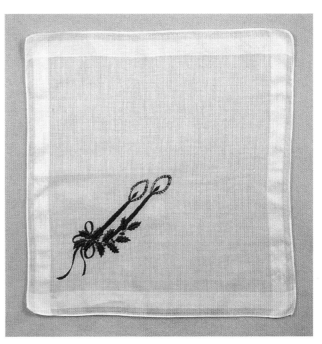

Tall red candles with leaves. $5-7.

A snowman clutches a long stem of red and white poinsettias. $5-7.

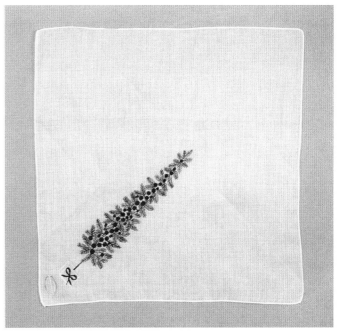

Tall thin Christmas tree. All cotton. Made in Switzerland. $5-7.

Long stem of poinsettias tied with ribbon. Tag reads: All cotton exclusive of decoration. Made in Switzerland. $5-7.

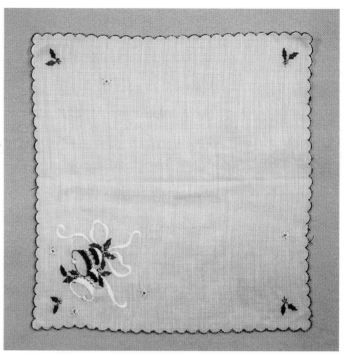

A white and red bell surrounded by pine branches. $5-7.

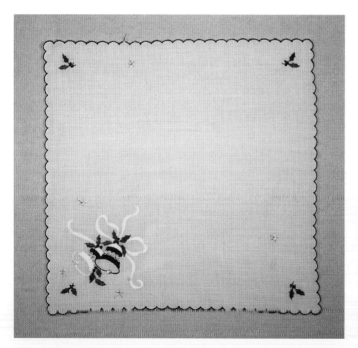

Pretty "ringing" bells with a touch of gold. $5-7.

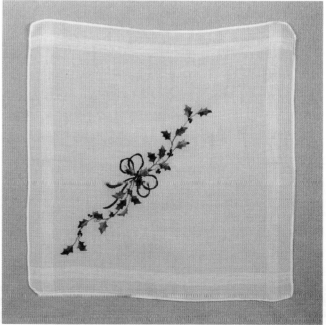

A sprig of holly tied with red ribbon. $5-7.

Poinsettias with red and yellow centers. Note the large design in one corner. $5-7.

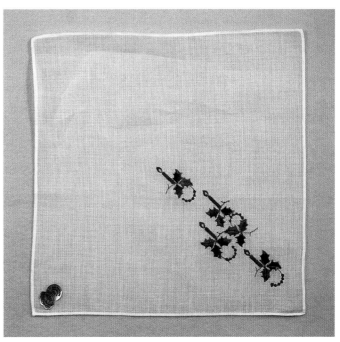

Red candles and green leaves. Tag reads: All cotton. Made in Switzerland. Desco. $5-7.

Red poinsettias and green stems. Red scalloped edge. $5-7.

Poinsettias and ribbon on a large hanky. One tag reads: Cocktail size. Other tag: All cotton. Made in Switzerland. $5-7.

Circular flowers on a white vine. $4-6.

Holly berries and leaves adorn this diminutive, lace-trimmed hanky. $5-7.

Red bells with green leaves. All cotton. Made in Switzerland. $5-7.

Red and white bell topped with white ribbon. $5-7.

Pretty little poinsettia tied with white ribbon. $3-5.

Simple design of holly berries. White crisscrossed ribbon makes this hanky different from many others. $5-7.

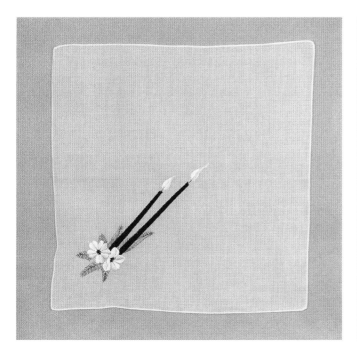

Tall red candles. White poinsettias and greens. $5-7.

Embroidered Christmas trees, one topped with a star. $5-7.

Red bells and lace adorn this cotton hanky. $5-7.

A candy cane "twist" on a common design. $5-7.

Santa Claus and Snowmen

What would Christmas be without Santa Claus and snowmen? Even people who live in warm climates enjoy images of snowmen at Christmas. These festive icons have made their way onto Christmas textiles and are among my favorites.

Red poinsettia. Ribbon border. $5-7.

Very pretty hanky trimmed with a border of bells and wreaths with candles, all joined with pink ribbon. Hand-painted Santas in corners. Small candles dot the center. Scalloped edges. $8-10.

Joyful Santas and ivy form the border of this hanky. $7-10.

Charming snow people decorate this unusual hanky. Red poinsettias adorn the corners. $8-10.

Jingle all the Way . . .

Melodious bells ring out on this group of hankies. Bells are a popular Christmas symbol.

Bells in various shapes and sizes. Red border. Synthetic. $7-10.

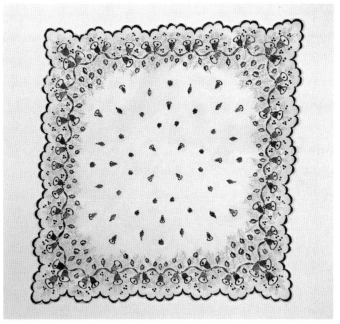

Chenille-like bells tied with ribbon form the border. Smaller bells in center. Synthetic. $7-10.

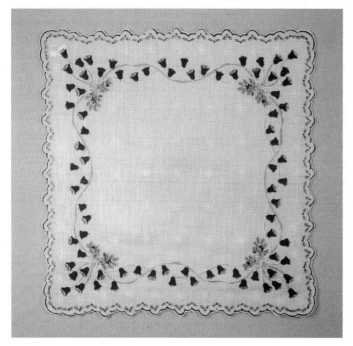

Strings of red bells, holly, and snowflakes adorn this hanky. Tag reads: A Burmel Original. $10-12.

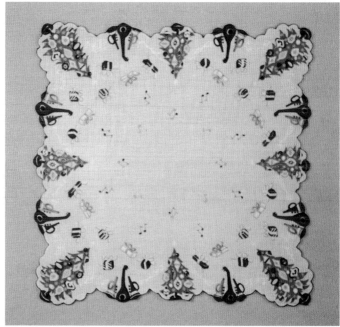

Delightful design of trees, musical instruments, gifts, and musical notes. $8-10.

O Tannenbaum

Apparently some hanky designers felt that one could not have a Christmas tree without musical accompaniment. Notice the way music is woven into these designs.

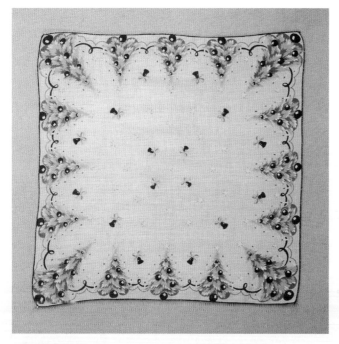

Charming Christmas trees with red ornaments and small red bells across center. *Courtesy of Karen A. Meer*. $8-10.

Mandolins, harps, and sheet music form the border of this hanky. Musical notes at center. $8-10.

Out in the Country . . .

These pretty handkerchiefs make us long for home with their idyllic country scenes.

Unusual design. Note the mill houses, trees, and snow. Pretty outer border of bells and inner design of poinsettias linked with ribbon. Truly lovely! $10-15.

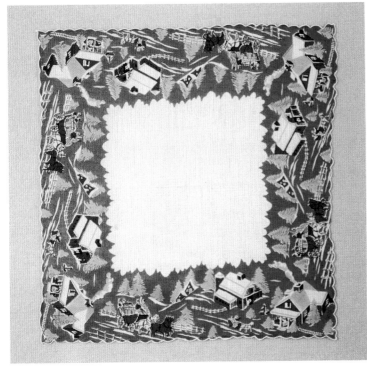

Interesting farm scene depicts red barns and horse-drawn carriages on a green ground. Ca. 1950-1960. $10-15.

Pretty border of yellow bells and clusters of holly. Musical notes waft from a family of carolers. Tag reads: Handkerchief of the month by Burmel. As seen in Vogue. $10-15.

Baubles and Bows

These sweet little numbers are decorated with packages, ornaments, and ribbons.

Unusual "squares" contain ornaments, pinecones, poinsettias, and snowflakes. $8-10.

Red and green ornaments are suspended from ivy. Ca. 1960s. $8-10.

Red candles are tied with red or green bows. $8-10.

Lanterns, sleighs, bells, holly, and pine branches edge this lovely handkerchief. Ca. 1960s. $8-10.

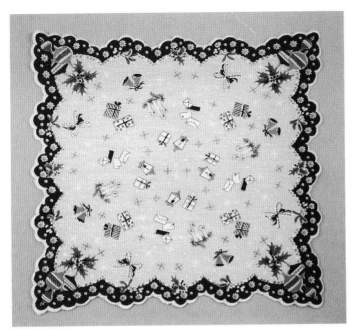

Charming motif of holly, presents, lanterns, and ornaments. Large ornaments in each corner and a red border. Scalloped edge. $10-12.

Very ornate. Large red bows and pinecone-trimmed wreaths enhance this beauty. Note the unusual center design. $10-12.

The Holly and the Ivy . . .

What could be more traditional than greenery at Christmas?

Clusters of holly encircle this hanky. $5-7.

Soft green wreaths and bells. Green edging. $5-8.

Bunches of holly and tiny poinsettias. Stripes of white ribbon in the cloth. $6-8.

Sprigs of Poinsettias

All of these hankies depict what I call "sprigs" of poinsettias, meaning each hanky has a large stem of poinsettias separate from the rest of the design.

Very large flowers and leaves make this hanky a knock-out. $8-10.

Oh, Those Poinsettias!

Poinsettias, poinsettias; the most common motif on Christmas hankies is a poinsettia. The theme may be traditional, but the way in which this Christmas flower is rendered often is not. While usually appearing in shades of red, they are sometimes seen in white or pink. Poinsettias show up on hankies in bouquets or singularly, scattered across the handkerchief or clustered in one corner. Some hankies have geometric shapes such as circles or squares to give them variety. Many poinsettia-bedecked hankies feature scalloped edges, but some are perfectly square. Cotton is the most common fabric, but some are made from synthetic materials. My favorite is the rare black handkerchief near the end of the group.

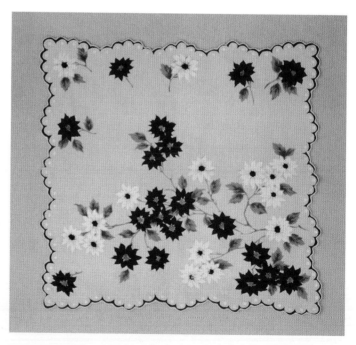

Red and white poinsettias on long stems. Pretty scalloped edge. *Courtesy of Karen A. Meer.* $8-10.

Poinsettia Bouquets

These poinsettias are rendered as bouquets.

Large red and white poinsettias. Holly border. Tag reads: All cotton. Philippine made. $8-10.

Poinsettia bouquets flourish in the corners of this hanky. Note the white "lace" and pale white flowers in the center. $10-12.

Large flowers and stems. $8-10.

Another hanky with bouquets of poinsettias on lace. Holly berries enhance the center. $10-12.

The hankies in this section all include circles in their designs.

Large central design of red and white poinsettias with light green and dark green leaves. White poinsettias on border. $10-12.

A square handkerchief with a border of poinsettias. Note the inner circle of gold and cream-colored snow flakes. $7-10.

A gorgeous hanky with poinsettias encircled by holly and berries. Note the holly chain all around the edge. $10-12.

A poinsettia border and a circle of poinsettias. $5-8.

A variation on the poinsettia border and the center circle. $5-8.

Vibrant poinsettias and a red and green wreath make this hanky delightful. $10-12.

A wide border of poinsettias creates a circle in the center of this hanky. Note the tiny red dots in the center. $8-10.

Poinsettias range from small to large on this hanky. $8-10.

Squared Off

There is nothing square about these handkerchiefs except their shapes!

A double row of poinsettias form the border. Small posies decorate the center. *Courtesy of Karen A. Meer.* $5-8.

Jolly snowmen dance in the center of this large hanky. $8-10.

A dense border of poinsettias with berries and leaves at the center. $5-8.

An unusual hanky with more green detail than most. Tag reads: All cotton. Made in Japan. $8-10.

Fit to Be Tied

The poinsettias on these lovely hankies are all tied with ribbons.

A wide border of poinsettias. $5-8.

Bouquets of red and white poinsettias are tied with ribbon. Very small bunches of berries in the center. $5-8.

Bunches of red poinsettias in each corner with white poinsettias in the center. $5-8.

Very pretty piece with large poinsettias, gold ribbon, and berries. $10-12.

A fancy edge and bunches of poinsettias tied with white ribbon. $5-8.

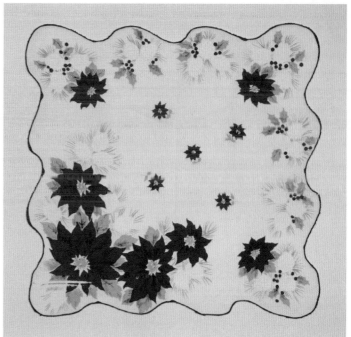

Large poinsettias with white pine cones and green leaves. $5-8.

Scallops, Anyone?

Scalloped edges add visual interest.

The gold on this hanky lends an elegant touch. Gold candles trim the border and cream-colored snowflakes enhance the center. $10-12.

Giant red poinsettias. Tag reads: Hand painted. All Cotton. Philippine made. $8-10.

Note the snowflake in the center and the lace-effect around the edge. $5-8.

Lovely scalloped edges and tiny posies enhance this hanky. $5-8.

Large and small poinsettias complement one another. $5-8.

Large flowers, stems, and leaves. Note the white leaves. $5-8.

Similar, But Not the Same!

These handkerchiefs are similar in design, but each has unique details.

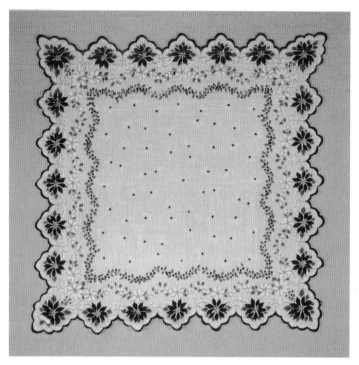

Rows of poinsettias and holly berries form the border. Small berries and white stems and leaves decorate the center. $5-8.

Unusual center design of leaves and berries. $5-8.

Lovely hanky with red and cream-colored poinsettias trimmed with gold. The gold snowflakes in the center add interest. $8-10.

Bunches of poinsettias are joined with gold ribbons. Note the cream-colored trees behind each cluster of poinsettias and the pretty border. $8-10.

Synthetics

These hankies are made from man-made materials. Notice the raised *chenille* poinsettias on the last handkerchief.

A synthetic hanky with raised, chenille-like flowers. $5-7.

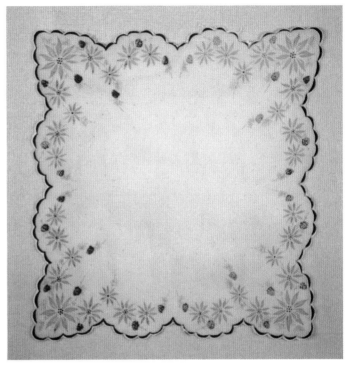

Nylon hanky with delicate flowers and pinecones around the border. $5-7.

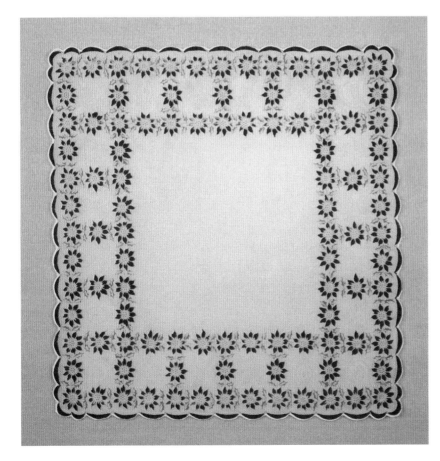

Candy canes, trees, and ornaments are outlined between poinsettias on this nylon hanky. $5-7.

Red and Green

The colors on these handkerchiefs are traditional Christmas colors.

Large poinsettias and bunches of holly, with red berries in center. $5-8.

Large poinsettias with unusual white pine cones. $5-8.

Poinsettias on a leafy vine make this square hanky cheery. $5-7.

This hanky has unusual touches of yellow on the poinsettia leaves. $8-10.

A beautiful hand-painted handkerchief. Deep red poinsettias with light green and dark green leaves. White flowers trim the border and center. $10-12.

Ribbons of poinsettias, candy canes, bells, and holly make for a lively mix. $5-8.

Large deep red poinsettias and clusters of small berries. $5-8.

An inner "square" of poinsettias and leaves mimics the outer design. $5-8.

A Bit of Blue

This handkerchief is unusual in its use of aqua-blue leaves and white poinsettias.

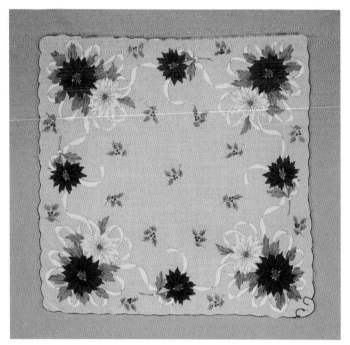

Turquoise leaves and white poinsettias make this hanky different. Clusters of flowers are linked with streamers of white ribbon. $8-10.

Bold and Beautiful

This striking handkerchief is a one-of-a-kind find. I love the "cut out" corner.

A cut-out corner design and a black background make this hanky truly unique. $10-15.

Orchids in Winter

While this handkerchief is not necessarily a Christmas handkerchief, its red and green colors and its beauty make it perfect for the holiday.

Christmas red orchids and green stems lend a festive air to this handkerchief. Hand rolled. *Courtesy of Karen A. Meer.* $10-12.

Hanky Boxes

Once-upon-a-time, hankies were presented as gifts in lovely handkerchief boxes. Sometimes, these boxes bore the name of the store where the hanky was purchased. Often the graphics on the box were fancier than the hankies themselves!

Jordan Marsh Company handkerchief box contains hanky. Colonial scene. Box reads: Joyous Merry Christmas. Ca. 1920s/1930s. $15-22.

Red box with picture of young skiers and terrier. Colonial scene in background. Note the space on the front of the box for "to and from." 10" square. Ca. 1920s/1930s. $15-20.

Beautiful embroidered bells embellish the hanky. Tag reads: All cotton. Made in Switzerland.

Poinsettia-trimmed hanky box. $8-12.

Adorable hanky box from Boston Store. Lettering reads: Wisconsin's Christmas City. Boston Store. Graphics consist of elves, Santa Claus, deer, and angels. Linen handkerchief inside. Ca. 1950s. $20-25.

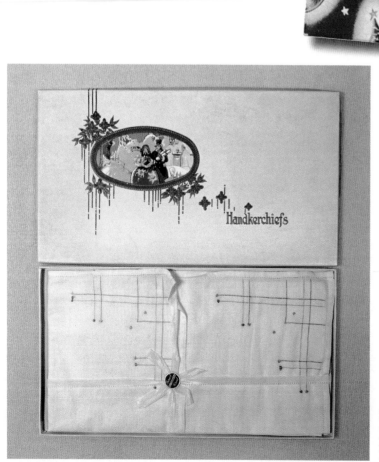

Deco-style box with colonial couple. *Handkerchiefs* written in gold script. The box contains two embroidered handkerchiefs tied with ribbon. Tag reads: Finest Hand Embroidery. Ca. 1920s/1930s. $18-22.

Hanky Cards

Handkerchiefs were sometimes attached to greeting cards. This section contains three examples: a handmade card; a vintage card; and a new example modeled after a vintage card.

Handmade greeting card is tied with ribbon and contains two handkerchiefs. Ca. 1940s. $10-15.

Sweet angel hangs ornament on tree. Her skirt is a handkerchief. $12-20.

Contemporary version of handkerchief greeting card. This paper doll wears a handkerchief dress and has a message written at the base. Made by *Two's Company*.
Doll wears a pink gown beneath the hanky. Ca. 2005. $15.

Fabric. Bark cloth-type pattern of poinsettias and pine cones. Cotton. $15-20.

Card Holders

Mail Call

Enjoy the vintage Christmas card holders made from felt that were popular in the 1960s. If you look closely at the magazine photo, you will see Santa's mail bag hanging on the Christmas tree. It is identical to the one my family had when I was a child.

A Santa mailbag hangs on a Christmas tree in this photo from *Better Homes & Gardens Ideas for Christmas 1964.*

Felt mail bag. Santa has a pompom on his hat and a pompom nose. This mailbag has been in my family since the early 1960s. $20-25.

Another adorable mail holder. A girl with a Christmas tree hat reaches out to collect the holiday mail. Felt. Ca. 1960s/1970s. $20-25.

Santa pops out of a red brick chimney to gather the mail. Felt. Ca. 1960s. *Courtesy of Victoria Michalets.* $20-25.

This Santa collects mail in his sleigh. Felt. Ca. 1960s. $20-25.

Christmas Stockings

The Stockings Were Hung . . .

Vintage Christmas stockings include those made from felt and fur. They were sewn from patterns and may also have been crocheted. Some Christmas stockings have images on both sides.

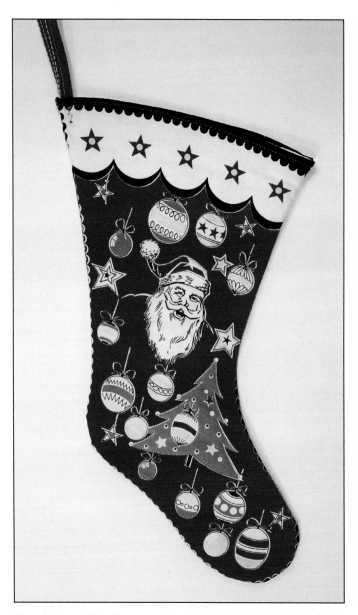

Two-sided stocking. Santa, trees, and ornaments on this side of this jazzy stocking. Ca. 1950s/1960s. $15-20.

Other side of stocking. Reads, "Merry Christmas."

Large fuzzy stocking with pompoms and bric-a-brac. Design in center suggests a sleigh. Ca. 1960s. $10-12.

Plush stocking with white trim. Felt deer trimmed in sequins. Jingle bell on toe. Ca. 1950s/1960s. $15-20.

Santa and snowflakes decorate this flannel stocking. Ca. 1960s. $10-15.

Printed cotton stocking. Santa waves as he stands next to his sleigh and reindeer. Ca. 1950s/1960s. $5-8.

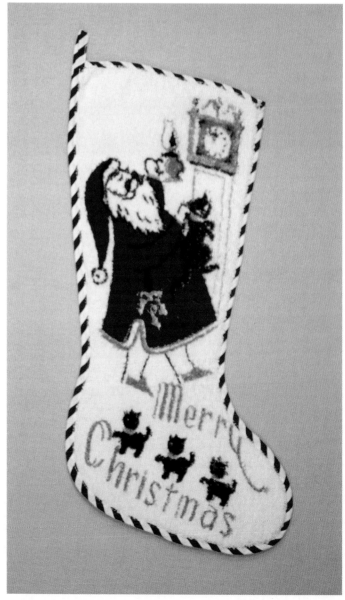

Santa in a sleeping gown is carrying a black cat on this terrycloth stocking. Note the cute black cats on the foot of the stocking. Ca. 1960s. $10-15.

Knitted stocking with furry Santa face, bells, and sequins. $8-12.

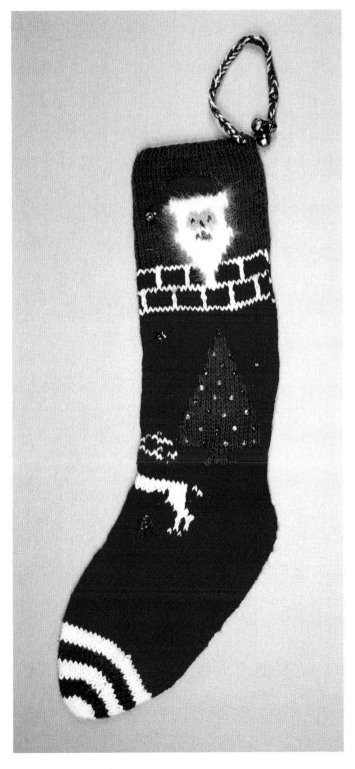

Quilted stocking with lace, felt, and sequin trim. $8-12.

Tree Skirts

Most of the vintage tree skirts I have come across are made from felt, including handmade styles. Felt tree skirts remain popular to this day. Some are quite lavish, with a lot of beading, cording, and ribbon trim. Magazines provided inspiration for making tree skirts and provided patterns that could be copied. Similar designs were used to make felt "table mats." My favorite is the cute cloth skirt at the end of the chapter. You've got to love those funky ornaments.

This pretty table mat is made from felt, of course! *Better Homes & Gardens Christmas Ideas for 1959.*

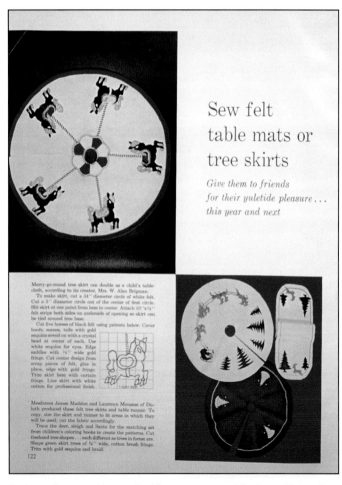

Patterns for tree skirts and table mats appeared in *Better Homes & Gardens Christmas Ideas for 1964.*

Snowmen frolic amid candy canes on this felt tree skirt trimmed with sequins. Ca.1960s. $30-40.

Tree skirt decorated with Santas, snowmen, and toys. Gold trim. Felt. Sticker on back reads: *Made in Japan.* Ca.1960s. $20-25.

Felt skirt with gold ornaments and large yellow bows. Snazzy braid trim. *Courtesy of Victoria Michalets.* $30-35.

Detail of bells and bow on tree skirt.

Santa, Christmas trees, and reindeer enliven this jazzy skirt with gold fringe. There are sequins, sequins, everywhere. Gold cord extends from Santa to reindeer. Ca.1960s. $30-35.

Gingerbread houses and gingerbread people adorn this cute skirt. Snowflakes are sequins. White yarn in a blanket stitch forms the hem. $30-40.

Santa goes down the chimney on this felt skirt.
Gold braid and fringe. Ca.1960s. $20-25.

Elves and trees make this
tree skirt cheery. Ca. 1960s.
$20-25.

White deer sport sequin-trimmed antlers on
this felt skirt. The snowflakes are made of paper.
Pompom fringe. Ca. 1950s/1960s. $30-40.

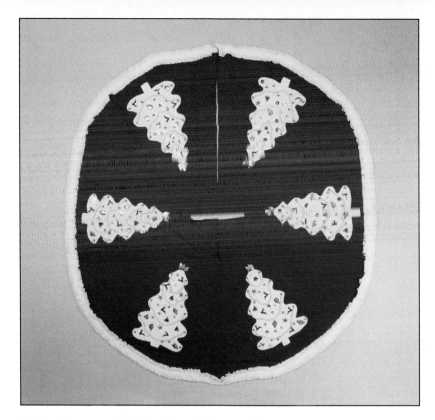

White felt trees on felt skirt. Lots of silver sequins accent this hand-sewn skirt. $25-30.

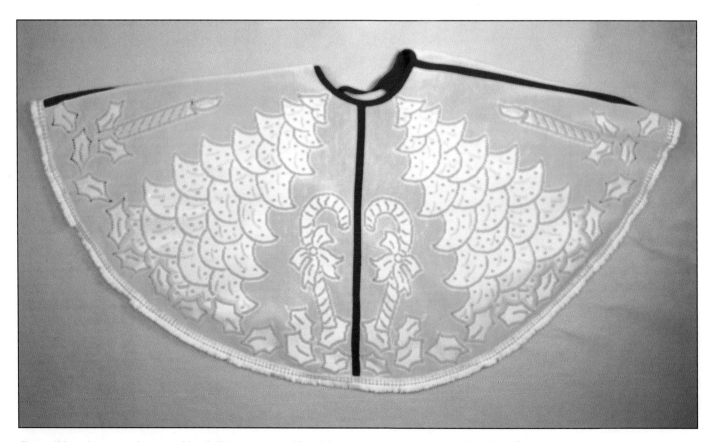

Reversible polyester and cotton skirt. Solid red on one side, white open-work on the other. Ca. 1970s. $20-25.

Large white poinsettias decorated with red sequins and gold beads accent this large skirt. Ca.1960s. $25-30.

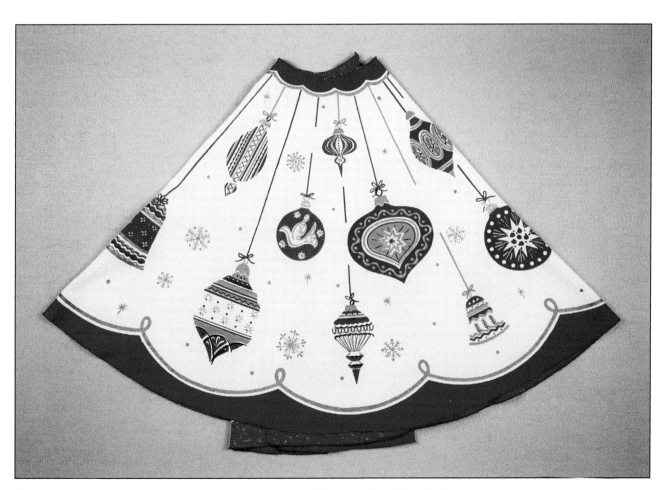

This skirt has a very mid-twentieth century look. Very cute. All cotton. Ca. 1950s. $25-30.

THE CHIRSTMAS FEAST

Red poinsettias, holly leaves, red berries. Cotton. $12-15.

Doilies and Table Runners

Delightful Doilies

Christmas doilies are not as prolific as other types of Christmas textiles. Since most doilies were crocheted, one knows they were intended for use at Christmas by their red and green color schemes. Some Christmas doilies remind me of snowflakes. My favorites are star-shaped cotton ones. The first one pictured is older, it is embroidered with a candle design, and it has a blanket stitch around the edges. The other doily is simpler with a machine-stamped design. There are many ways one can use doilies during the Christmas holiday season. Wouldn't a crocheted doily look pretty lining a basket of edible holiday treats? Let imagination be your guide.

Crocheted Cuties

Delicate red and green doily with white fringe edge. $8-12.

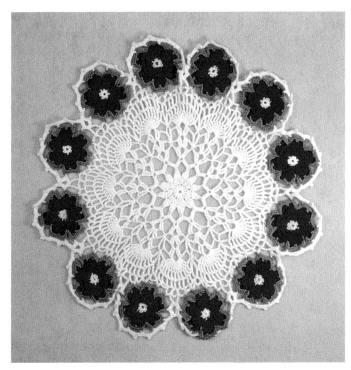

Crocheted doily with beautiful white center and colorful "mini poinsettias" on the outside. $8-12.

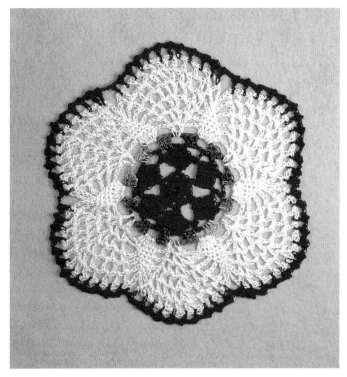

Delicate crocheted doily trimmed with red. Red and green center. $8-12.

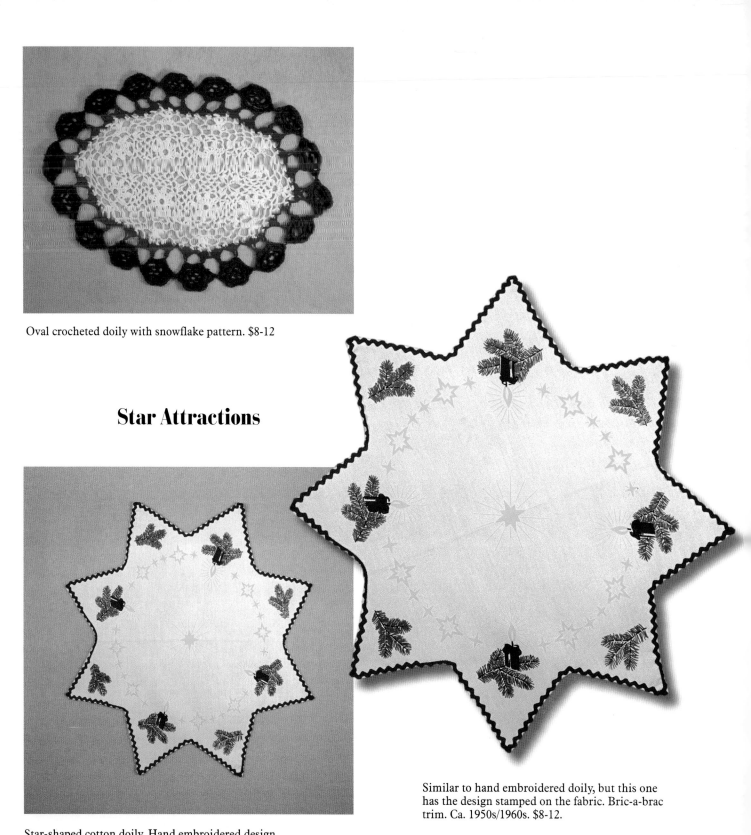

Oval crocheted doily with snowflake pattern. $8-12

Star Attractions

Star-shaped cotton doily. Hand embroidered design of candles on pine boughs. $13-18.

Similar to hand embroidered doily, but this one has the design stamped on the fabric. Bric-a-brac trim. Ca. 1950s/1960s. $8-12.

More Delightful Doilies

Felt doily with gold braid trim and holly berries. Probably homemade. $8-12.

This doily has a Scandinavian design of hearts, tulips, and pine boughs. $13-17.

Christmas Runners

I love vintage Christmas table runners, especially those dating from the 1930s and 1940s. Their bold colors and quaint village scenes speak to me. Every year, I use the oval runner with song lyrics beneath a group of like-colored snowmen. I also love everything with bells

Darling oval table scarf with colonial people and village scene. Colors are very representative of the 1930s era. Ca.1920s/1930s. $30-40.

Detail of oval table scarf.

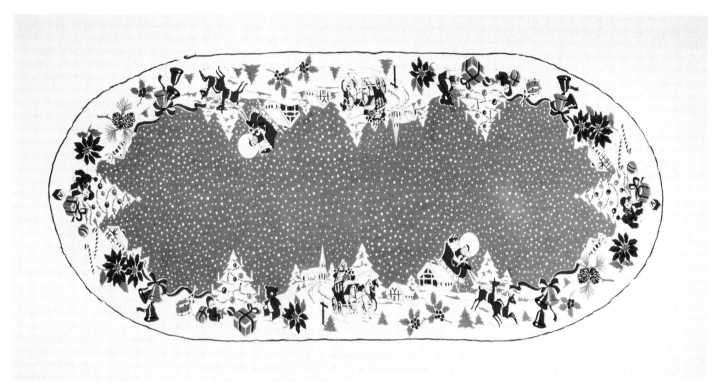

Charming oval table runner. Santa Claus makes an appearance on this red, white, and green scarf. Ca. 1940s. $25-35.

A flamboyant runner complete with song lyrics, horse-drawn carriages, sleigh bells, people, houses, musical notes, Santa Claus, and holly! 16"x42". Ca. 1950s/1960s. $30-40.

Bright and bold runner in shades of red, blue, and yellow. Old-fashioned people and images of Santa Claus. Ca. 1930s/1940s. $30-$40.

Classic linen runner with chiming red and white bells, holly berries, and gold stars. 16"x47". Ca. 1940s. $25-35.

Cotton runner with large gold candles in red bases, encircled with evergreens. Border of red ribbon and ornaments. 19"x39". Ca. 1950s/1960s. $20-30.

Elegant cotton runner with red and gold bells. Ca. 1940s. $25-35.

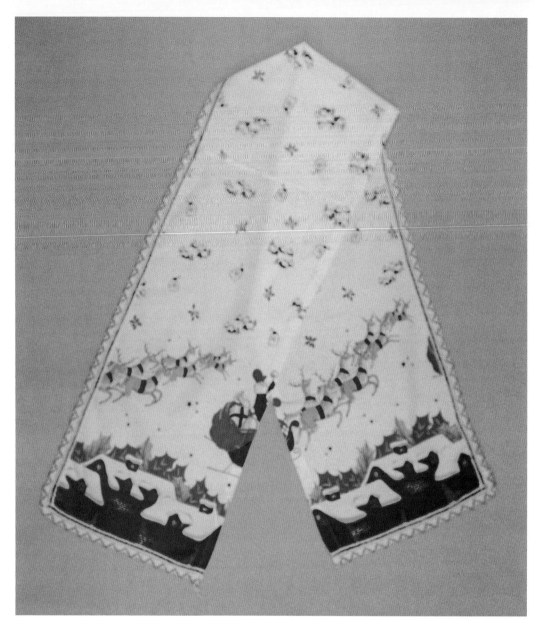

Table runner made from vintage fabric depicts Santa and his reindeer. $10-15.

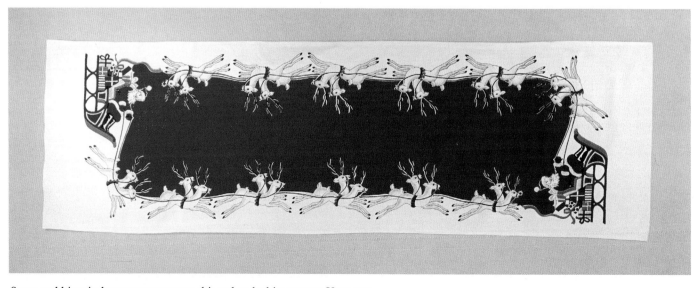

Santa and his reindeer scamper across this red and white runner. Very cute.
Ca. 1950s/1960s. *Courtesy of Shari Lautenbach.* $25-35.

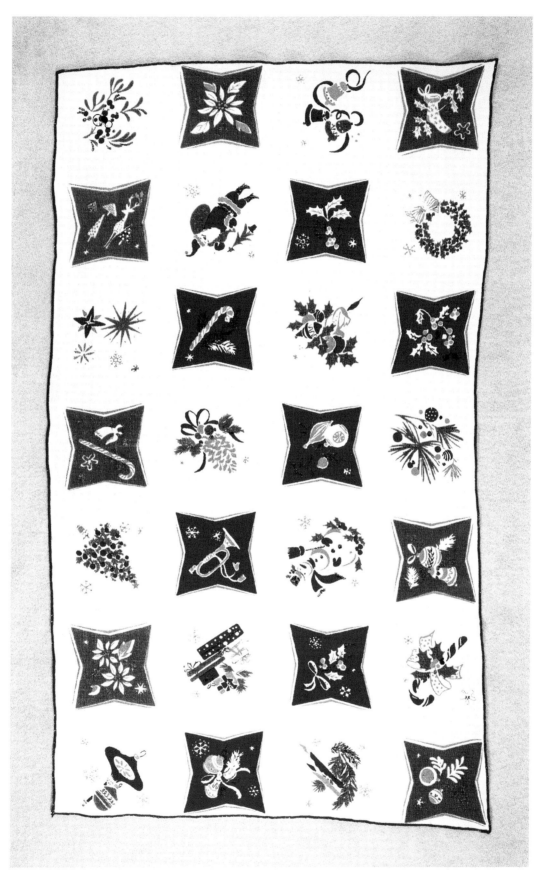

Linen runner features star-shaped designs, bells, ornaments, Santas, Christmas trees, and more. Very 1950s! $15-20.

Vintage Embroidery

These are two of my earliest purchases. I use the first one, of unusual shape, on the top of the tank in the bathroom. The shape of the scarf fits the space so well. The second one has a lovely tatted edge.

Dresser scarf with an irregular shape. Finely embroidered poinsettias and leaves. Note the crocheted edge. $20-30.

Dresser scarf. Unusual green embroidered vases are filled with red poinsettias. Lovely lace edge. $20-30.

God Jul

Who wouldn't enjoy a Christmas meal with these pretty table runners?

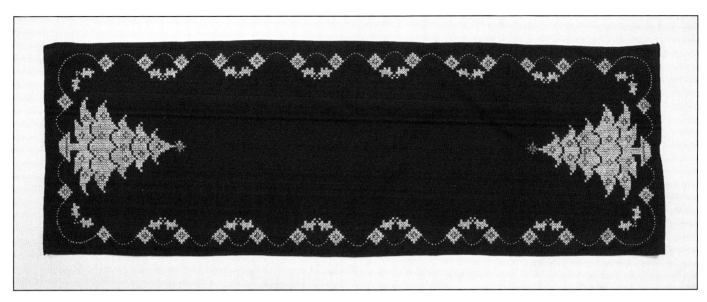

Red table runner with white cross-stitched trees. $15-20.

This runner wishes " A Merry Christmas" in Norwegian/Swedish. $12-18.

More Poinsettias

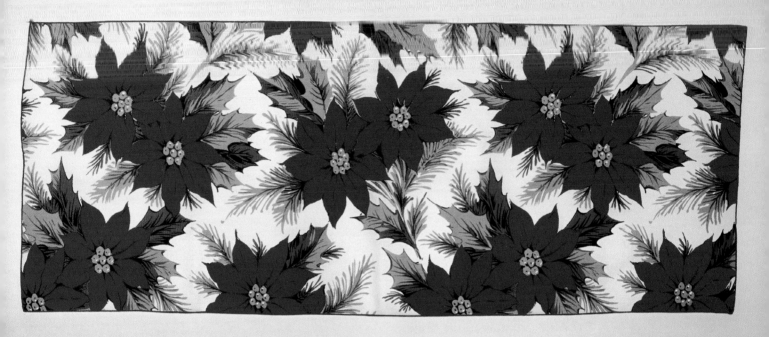

Cotton table runner with vibrant poinsettias and leaves. Ca. 1960s/1970s. $15-20.

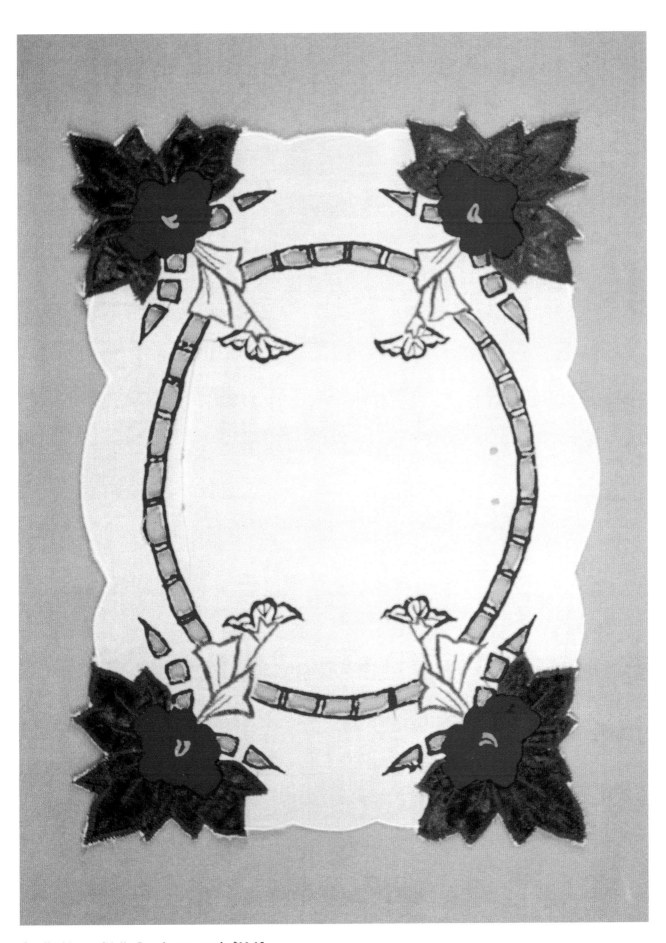

Small table scarf/doily. Lovely open work. $10-15.

Tablecloths

Traditional Motifs

Vintage Christmas tablecloths may be found in many sizes, shapes, and styles. They were very popular in the 1940s, often being decorated with that era's popular poinsettias, candles, bells, holly, wreaths, and ornaments. They are generally made of cotton and may have survived for so many years because they were used just once a year. It is amazing to see how many ways poinsettias and candles can be depicted. Most of the tablecloths shown in this chapter are machine-made, but some are homemade and hand-embroidered.

Grandma's Pride

A border of sleighs, bells, poinsettias, and gifts decorate this cotton, rectangular cloth. Bells strung on garland decorate the center. Cotton. 46" x 50". Ca. 1960s. $25-35.

Pretty design of ribbons, bells, candy jars, presents, and drums. Cotton. 42" x 52". Ca. 1960s/1970s. $25-35.

Clusters of ornaments and pine cones strung on red ribbon.
Cotton. 58" x 92". Ca. 1960s. $25-35.

Elegant design of baskets, candles, pitchers, and glass dishes filled with greens, poinsettias, and ornaments. Solid red center. Cotton. 58" x 72". Ca. 1960s. $30-40.

Large silver candles, silver ornaments, and red poinsettias with black veins. 50"x 60". Cotton. Ca. 1940s. $25-35.

An unusual tablecloth. Clusters of holly leaves are secured with red ribbon. An unusual center design of red and gold bells. Cotton. 50" x 58". Ca. 1940s/1950s. $ 30-40.

This tablecloth sports a wide border of wreaths, bells, and ribbons. Center design of poinsettias, ornaments, and bells. Cotton. 56" x 72". Ca. 1960s. $25-35.

Large red, green, and gold bells accent the corners of this bright cloth, with clusters of poinsettias in between. Center design of small bells and holly. Cotton. 42" x 50". Ca. 1940s/1950s. $25-35.

Hints of orange-gold in this tablecloth set it apart from others. Cotton. $25-35.

Ribbon-tied wreaths, small Christmas trees, and jingling bells outline this cloth. The center features a design of holly and poinsettias. Cotton. *Courtesy* of *Kirsti Hoffman.* Ca.1960s. $25-35.

Old time lanterns and colonial-style bells give this tablecloth a different flare. Cotton. 52" x 56". $25-35.

Trios of red candles tied with red ribbon. Bells in center. Cotton. 46" x 50". Ca. 1960s. $25-35.

Vibrant gold candles and red poinsettias on white
cotton. Gray branches. 52" x 66". $30-35.

Red bows, pine cones, and holly leaves. Red edging.
Cotton. 50" x 68". $22-27.

Very large tablecloth. Unusual design of red and black stripes in center. Ornaments and pine branches border the stripes. Cotton. 60" x 80". Ca. 1960s. $40-45.

Clusters of ornaments on holly leaves. Cotton. 50" x 60". Ca.1960s. $22-27.

Squares outlined with snowflakes contain pine cones, ornaments, bells, holly, and candles accented with green boughs. Cotton. 48" x 60". Ca. 1960s. $25-35.

Candy canes are tied with red ribbon. Pretty center pattern. Cotton. 50" x 62". $25-35.

Red bells in the corners as well as trios of red candles along the sides.
Thin red ribbon outlines the cloth. Cotton. Ca.1960s. 50" x 56". $25-35.

Very nostalgic tablecloth. "Boxes" of red and white are filled with snowmen, reindeer, bells, and Christmas trees. Center design of holly berries. Fun and unusual! Cotton. 52" x 56". Ca. 1950s. $30-40.

Detail of quaint bells and house.

Detail of several panels.

This cloth reads, "Merry Christmas" along the border. Santa and his reindeer fly across the center. Cotton. 23" x 42". Ca. 1950s/1960s. $30-40.

Trios of minstrels serenade on this synthetic tablecloth. 50" x 68". Ca. 1960s/1970s. $30-40.

This tablecloth reminds me of "Whoville" in the Dr. Seuss classic, *The Grinch Who Stole Christmas*! Truly unique. Cotton. 60" x 64" Ca. 1960s. $30-40.

Dark green trees are laden with toys and ornaments. Cotton. 60" x 72". Ca.1960s/1970s. $25-35.

These small cloths are of cardtable size.

Small square cloth. Yellow and red stars decorate the center of this little cutie featuring pine boughs and candles. Cotton. 28" square. $18-25.

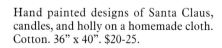

Hand painted designs of Santa Claus, candles, and holly on a homemade cloth. Cotton. 36" x 40". $20-25.

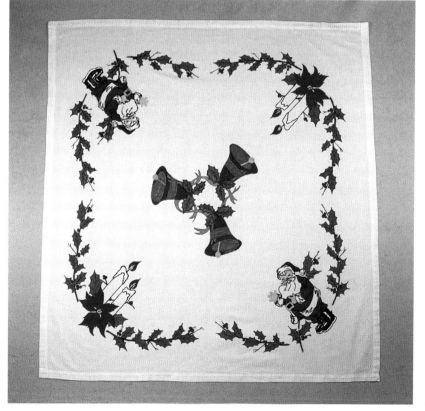

Roundabout

Christmas tablecloths come in round and oval shapes, as well as rectangular and square shapes. Some round tablecloths are decorated with fringe.

Victorian-style people decorate this round, fringe-trimmed cloth. It was one of my first Christmas tablecloths. I use it as a tree skirt. Cotton. Ca.1940s. $30-40.

Round tablecloth edged with fringe. Striking poinsettias and candles. Ca. 1960s/1970s. $30-40.

Large red poinsettias. Red border. Ca. 1970s. $25-35.

An intricate border and detailed center make this tablecloth a keeper.
Cotton. Ca. 1960s. $30-40.

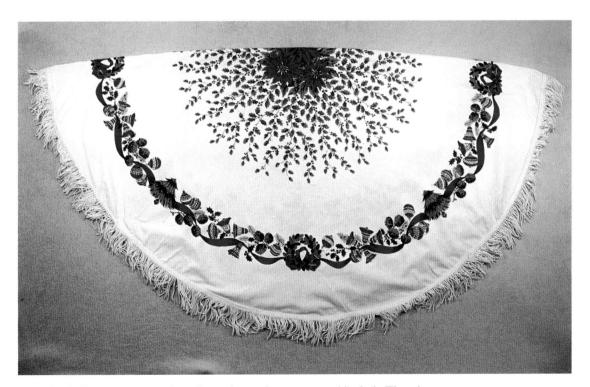

Wreaths, bells, ornaments, and candles make up the pattern on this cloth. There is a
large center design of holly. Red ribbon and white fringe. Cotton. $30-40.

Ornaments, holly, and pine boughs are entwined on this fringe-trimmed tablecloth. Unusual center design of a red circle and gold, black, and white stars. Cotton. Ca. 1960s. $25-35.

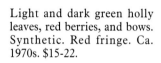

Light and dark green holly leaves, red berries, and bows. Synthetic. Red fringe. Ca. 1970s. $15-22.

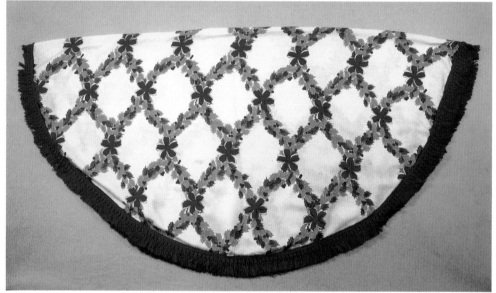

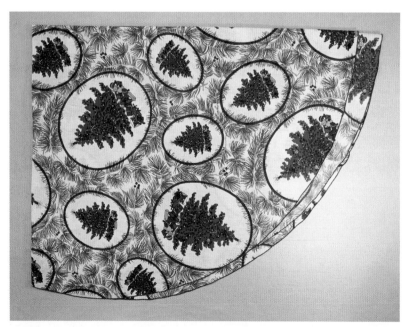

Lightweight oval cloth. Tree and gift motif. Cotton. *Courtesy of Kirsti Hoffman.* Ca.1970s. $15-20.

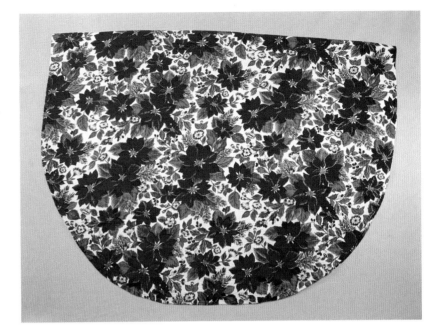

Red poinsettias with gold accents.
Oval. Ca.1970s. $15-18.

Center design of poinsettias and leaves. Red
border. Cotton. Ca. 1970s. $20-25.

Closely clustered poinsettias and leaves.
Red Border. Cotton. $20-25.

Vera Tablecloths

Vera Neuman designed Christmas tablecloths as well as tablecloths with floral and geometric designs. Her tablecloths are in demand by collectors.

Vera design. Non-traditional red and green tablecloth. Cotton. Ca. 1970s. $35-40.

Holly and bows. Red fringe border. Synthetic. Ca.1970s. $20-25.

Seeing Red. . .

These tablecloths are primarily red in color or have a red center. Nothing says Christmas like the color red.

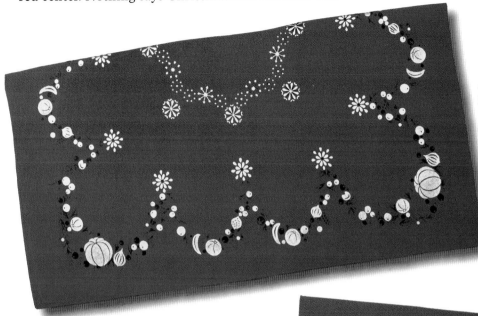

A Christmas harvest of snowflakes and pumpkins. Cotton. 48" square. $25-30.

Large red cotton cloth. Gold and dark red poinsettias and gold trim. 52" x 80". $30-35.

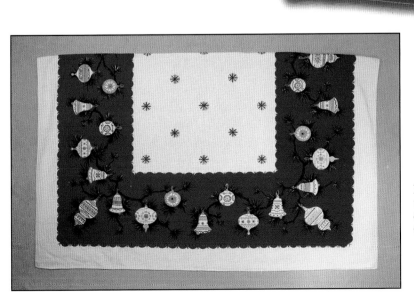

Heavy linen cloth with white center dotted with colored snowflakes. Wide design of red with white and gold snowflakes. Cotton. Ca. 1950s/1960s. $30-40.

Candles, trees, lanterns, and ornaments trim this tablecloth. A red ribbon motif is used throughout. Solid red center. Cotton. 46" x 60". Ca. 1950s/1960s. $30-40.

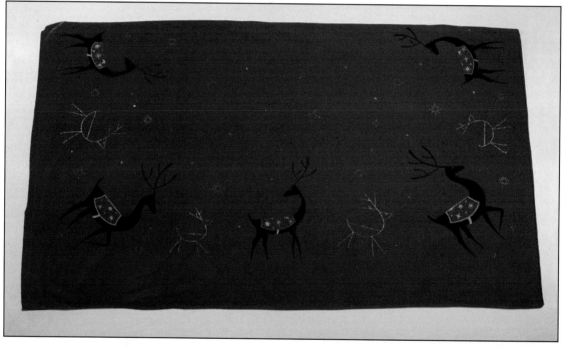

Very large and very modernistic piece. Black and silver deer. Gold and silver snowflakes. Ca. 1960s. *Courtesy of Ellen Michalets.* $25-35.

Detail of a deer.

A different type of cloth with large green bells on red. Red and green candy canes. Cotton. 50" x 58". Ca.1940s. $25-35.

Holly leaves and white and red berries. Cotton. 52" x 60". $18-25.

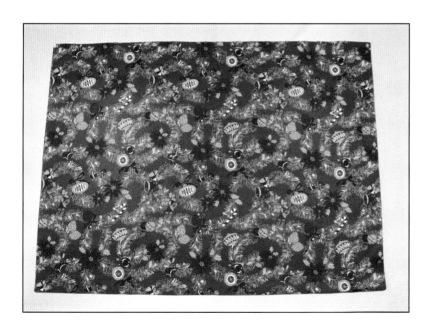

Green garland bedecked with baubles, candy canes, and pine cones. Note the avocado green tone of this 1970s tablecloth. Cotton. 56" x 82". $30-35.

. . . and Green

What is red without green at Christmas?

Holly, ribbons, and berries trim this tablecloth. Ring of holly in the center. Cotton. 56" x 80". Linen. $25-30.

This unusual cloth depicts an entire Christmas scene: tree, gifts, red door, cats, presents. Very cute! Synthetic. 58" x 80". Ca. 1970s. $25-35.

Green linen with pinecone and snowflake design. Tag reads: *California Hand Prints. Reg.
U.S. Pat. Off.* Cotton. 46" x 52". Ca. 1960s. $22-27.

Holly on light and dark
green background with red
fringe. Synthetic mate-
rial. 56" square. Ca. 1970s.
$15-20.

Mesh table covering with pompom trim. Felt
bells and metal jingle bells. $12-15

Did You Say "Poinsettias"?

Poinsettias were a very popular motif for tablecloths.

Border of poinsettias and green garland tied with red ribbons. Green garland in
center. Synthetic. 50" square. $25-30.

Large rectangular cloth with red poinsettia border. Cotton. $25-30.

Large red poinsettias with mint-green leaves and holly. Cotton. 33" x 50". $25-30.

Groupings of three red candles, large holly leaves, and pine cones decorate this elegant cloth. Cotton. 58" x 60". Ca. 1960s. $30-40.

Bows and poinsettias rim this cloth. A beribboned circle of holly decorates the center. Cotton, 44" x 50", ca. 1960s. $25-30.

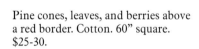

Pine cones, leaves, and berries above a red border. Cotton. 60" square. $25-30.

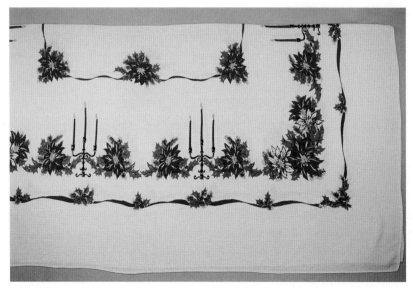

Elegant tablecloth with poinsettias and candles among evergreens. Center design of poinsettias linked with ribbon. Cotton. 50" x 64". $30-40.

146

Bundles of red and pink poinsettias along red ribbons. Cotton. 56" x 96". $30-35.

Round cloth. Silver candles, green, red, and white ornaments. White fringe. Cotton. Very attractive. Ca. 1960s. $25-35.

Large poinsettias, candles, and ribbon accent this pretty cloth. Cotton. 60" x 88". $25-35.

147

Very large rectangular cloth. Unusual design of poinsettias and fruit. Ca. 1970s. *Courtesy of Victoria Michalets.* $25-35.

Red poinsettias and red bells, all joined with a red ribbon. Red center. Cotton. 60" x 80". Ca.1940s/1950s. $35-40.

This tablecloth features white poinsettias along with the red ones. Holly and bells decorate the outside, while the center is solid green. Cotton. Ca. 1940s. *Courtesy of Shari Lautenbach.* $25-35.

Lovely silver candles appear between corner bouquets. Design of red and green leaves in center. Cotton. $30-40.

Gold candles and red and white ornaments. Green leaves. Cotton. 52" x 62". Circa 1950s. $25-35.

Bauble-trimmed beauty. Cotton. 24" x 44". Circa 1960s. $25-35.

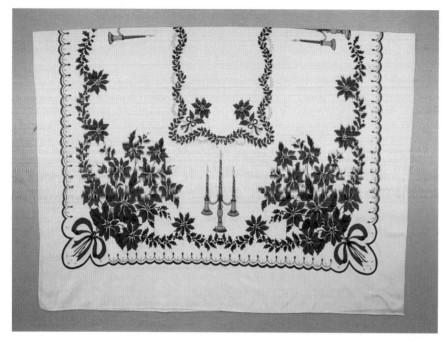

A gorgeous tablecloth with striped candles, poinsettias and an unusual center design. Cotton. 43" x 60". $30-40.

Red border contains gold, black, and white snowflakes. Red poinsettias and holly berries in center. Cotton. 46" x 50". $22-28.

Candles, poinsettias, and ornaments, this tablecloth has it all. Cotton. Ca. 1960s. $30-40.

Traditional poinsettias and bells. Cotton. 60" x 68". Ca. 1960s. $22-28.

Small homemade table cloth. Red poinsettias and green ribbons. Cotton. $12-15.

Embroidered Beauties

Embroidered tablecloths feature more subtle designs. The lovely tablecloth with red bells comes with a set of embroidered napkins.

Detail of cross-stitched bells.

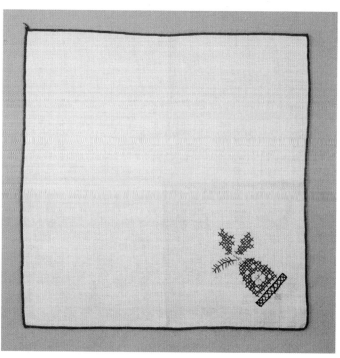

Coordinating napkin. Set of 8, $40.

A card table cloth. Lovely red and white cross-stitched bells are linked with green ribbon. Note the small rhinestones on the bell clappers. Linen. $25-35.

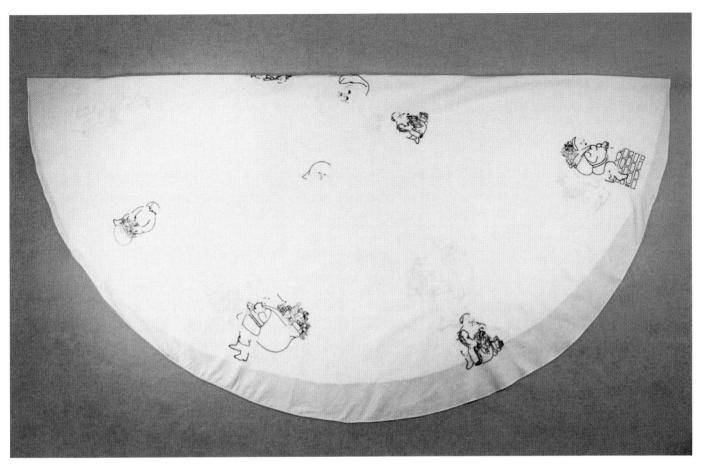

Round tablecloth with embroidered Santa Claus. Cotton. $22-28.

Detail of Santa with his pack and Christmas tree.

Santa with a bag of goodies.

Santa checks his list.

Santa hauls a heavy load.

Napkins

Nice and Neat

Some napkins came as a set with tablecloths. Today, most of these are now "loners."

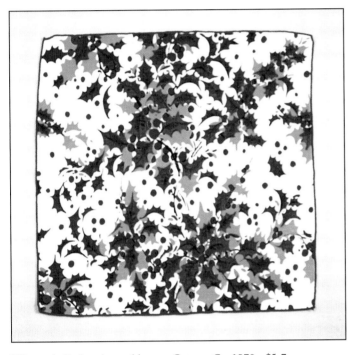

Vibrant holly berries and leaves. Cotton. Ca. 1970s. $5-7.

Country patchwork design. Ca.1970s. Cotton. $5-7.

Bold red poinsettias with checked bows. Cotton. $5-7.

Center wreath encircled by red and gold ornaments.
Cotton. Ca. 1960s. $5-7.

Paisley design in red and green. Cotton. Ca. 1970s. $5-7.

Small napkin with "Season's Greetings". Cotton.
Courtesy of Shari Lautenbach. $4-6.

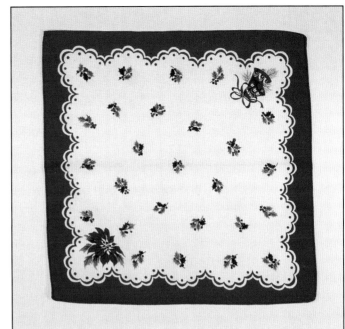

Red bells and a poinsettia in a snowflake design. Cotton. $5-7.

Four different designs. Angels, Santas, ornaments, bells, and more. Very mid-twentieth century! Cotton. Set of 8. $16-24.

A large bouquet and three small ones joined by a red ribbon. Cotton. $5-7.

Bird napkins with a Christmas motif. Cotton. $6 each.

Detail of napkin with blue jay.